18th Edition

Aerofilms Guide

FOOTBALL
GROUNDS

Fully Revised for the **2010/2011** Season and featuring every
Barclays Premier League and npower League Club

18th Edition

Aerofilms Guide

FOOTBALL
GROUNDS

Fully Revised for the **2010/2011** Season and featuring every
Barclays Premier League and npower League Club

Ian Allan
PUBLISHING

CONTENTS

Front cover, from left to right:
Molineux Ground (Wolverhampton Wanderers, 703113); Glanford Park (Scunthorpe United, 702971); Huish Park (Yeovil Town, 702785); Kassam Stadium (Oxford United, 703042).

Back cover, from left to right:
Britannia Stadium (Stoke City, 703102); Carrow Road (Norwich City, 702870); Edgar Street (Hereford United, 703025); KRBS Priestfield Stadium (Gillingham, 702847).

First published 2010

Reprinted 1993 (twice); Second edition 1994; Third edition 1995; Fourth edition 1996; Fifth edition 1997; Sixth edition 1998; Seventh edition 1999; Eighth edition 2000; Ninth edition 2001; Tenth edition 2002; 11th edition 2003, reprinted 2003. 12th edition 2004; 13th edition 2005; 14th edition 2006; 15th edition 2007; 16th edition 2008; 17th edition 2009; 18th edition 2010

ISBN 978 0 7110 3534 8

Published by Ian Allan Publishing

an imprint of Ian Allan Publishing Ltd, Hersham, Surrey KT12 4RG.
Printed by Ian Allan Printing Ltd, Hersham, Surrey KT12 4RG.

Text © Ian Allan Publishing Ltd 1993-2010
Diagrams © Ian Allan Publishing Ltd 2000-2010
Aerial Photography © Blom Aerofilms 1993-2010

Mixed Sources
Product group from well-managed forests and other controlled sources
www.fsc.org Cert no. SGS-COC-005526
© 1996 Forest Stewardship Council
FSC

Visit the Ian Allan Publishing web site at www.ianallanpublishing.com

INTRODUCTION

Welcome to the 18th edition of *Aerofilms Guide: Football Grounds*. As with the previous editions, we have endeavoured to update the book to reflect all of the latest changes to Premier and Football League grounds since the publication of the last edition 12 months ago.

For the new season, there are two new grounds to record at League clubs. For both Chesterfield and Morecambe the new season will bring home fixtures at new stadia; for Chesterfield in particular the move to the new b2net Stadium marks the end of more than 100 years at Saltergate. Of the 92 clubs comprising the top four divisions in English football, about one third have now moved grounds over the past 20 years and the pace of relocation seems to be accelerating as new grounds are either under construction or proposed for almost a further 10 teams. Moreover of those clubs that have not relocated, the vast majority now play in stadia that have been radically transformed since the twin disasters of Valley Parade and Hillsborough.

Coming up from the Blue Square Premier League are two clubs, only one of which has played host to League football in the past. This is Oxford United, a club that returns to the Football League after an absence of four years. The second team to come up is Stevenage, which finally gains League status after several years of nearly achieving it. Promotion from the top-flight of non-League football for two clubs means relegation for two others and, at the end of the 2009/10 season, Darlington and Grimsby Town both failed to survive, the former losing its League status for the second time after going into Administration during the 2008/09 season.

During the course of the 2009/10 season two teams – Crystal Palace and Portsmouth – entered Administration and suffered the consequent deduction of points. Other clubs – such as Accrington Stanley, Cardiff City and Southend United – were all subject to action in the courts by HM Revenue & Customs over unpaid tax whilst several other clubs also seem to be less financially secure than their fans would hope. Over the past 20 years football has benefited from a huge financial boost, some of which has gone to fund new building work and facilities but much of which has gone to pay the ever-increasing salaries of the top players. With financial stringency now the watchwords alongside the high level of debt carried by some of the highest-profile clubs in the country, it's unlikely that the two teams that succumbed to Administration in 2009/10 will be the last.

As always the editorial team hopes that you will have an enjoyable season and that your particular team achieves the success that you, as fans, think that it deserves. We trust that, whatever the season ultimately holds for your team, that you will make the most of the opportunities that the season has to offer.

We also hope that you will find this guide of use. As always, please e-mail any comments or corrections to the editor at info@ianallanpublishing.co.uk

Disabled Facilities

We endeavour to list the facilities for disabled spectators at each ground. Readers will appreciate that these facilities can vary in number and quality and that, for most clubs, pre-booking is essential. Some clubs also have dedicated parking for disabled spectators; this again should be pre-booked if available.

Blom Aerofilms Ltd

Blom Aerofilms is one of the UK's leading providers of aerial photography and digital map solutions for civil engineering design, environmental assessment and land information management. The company provides a complete range of mapping services including aerial photography, GIS base mapping, orthophoto production, geo-spatial solutions and airborne laser-scanning.

wembley

Wembley Stadium, Wembley National Stadium Ltd, Wembley Way, London HA9 0WS

website: **WWW.WEMBLEYSTADIUM.COM**
tel no: **0844 980 8001**

Fax: 020 8795 5050

Brief History: Inaugurated for the FA Cup Final of 1923, venue for many national and international matches including the World Cup Final of 1966. Also traditionally used for other major sporting events and as a venue for rock concerts and other entertainments. The original Wembley with its twin towers was demolished in 2002 when work started on the construction of the new ground. After some delay, the new Wembley was completed in the spring of 2007 with its first major match being the FA Cup Final in May 2007. Record attendance at original Wembley: 126,047; at rebuilt ground: 89,826

(Total) Current Capacity: 90,000 (all-seated)

Visiting Supporters' Allocation: not applicable

Nearest Railway Station: Wembley Complex (Network Rail), Wembley Central (Network Rail and London Underground) and Wembley Park (London Underground)

Parking (Car): Very limited at the ground with residents' only schemes in adjacent housing areas.

Parking (Coach/Bus): As directed

Police Force: Metropolitan (0300 123 1212)

Disabled Visitors' Facilities:
Wheelchairs: 310 spaces for wheelchair-bound fans throughout the ground
Blind: To be confirmed

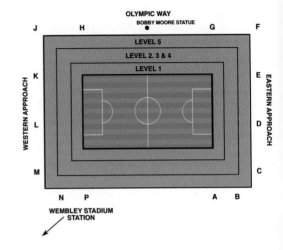

1 Olympic Way
2 Statue of Bobby Moore
3 To Wembley Park station
4 Wembley Complex
    railway station
5 To London Marylebone
6 To Wembley Central
7 Eastern Approach
8 Turnstiles 'G'
9 Turnstiles 'H'
10 Turnstiles 'F'
11 Turnstiles 'E'
12 Turnstiles 'D'

↑ North direction (approx)

◄ 701519
▼ 701513

accrington stanley

Fraser Eagle Stadium, Livingstone Road, Accrington, Lancashire BB5 5BX

website: **WWW.ACCRINGTONSTANLEY.CO.UK**
e:mail: **INFORMATION@ACCRINGTONSTANLEY.CO.UK**
tel no: **0871 4341968**
colours: **RED SHIRTS, RED SHORTS**
nickname: **THE REDS, STANLEY**
season 2010/11: **LEAGUE TWO**

Last Season: **15th (p46; w18; d7; l21; gf62; ga74)**

It's almost 50 years since the original Accrington Stanley was forced out of the Football League as a result of financial problems and, during the course of the 2009/10 season, it looked for a period as though history was going to repeat itself as the club faced a winding up order for more than £300,000 of unpaid tax. However, a combination of fund raising and the arrival of a local saviour in Ilyas Khan resulted in the threat being lifted. On the field, the club prospered for much of the season and seemed to have a reasonable chance of making the Play-Offs in mid-March when the team stood in ninth place, two points off the Play-Offs but with games in hand. However, a late loss of form saw the team take only eight points from the final 12 League matches to end up in a disappointing 15th place. Away from the League, John Coleman's side claimed the scalp of League One Walsall in the first round of the Carling Cup. For the new season, although Ilyas Khan has stood down as chairman he has vowed to continue his financial backing of the club and so, with financial stability assured, Coleman should be able to plan for the new season with more confidence. A top-half finish should certainly be a possibility but the Play-Offs may be unrealistic given the ambition of a number of other teams in this division.

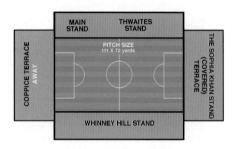

Advance Tickets Tel No: 01254 356950
Fax: 01254 356951
Training Ground: King George V Playing Fields, Royds Avenue, Accrington BB5 2JX
Brief History: The original club was formed as Accrington Villa in 1891, becoming Accrington Stanley in 1895. The team entered the Football League in 1921 and remained a member until its resignation in 1962. Following four years outside the League, the original club folded in 1966 and was not resurrected until 1970. The club has been based at the Crown Ground (now called the Fraser Eagle Stadium) since it was reformed but prior to 1966 the original club played at Peel Park, which is now demolished. Record Attendance (at Fraser Eagle Stadium) 4,368

(Total) Current Capacity: 5,057 (2,000 seated)
Visiting Supporters' Allocation: 1,500 on uncovered Coppice Terrace plus part of covered Whinney Hill Stand if required
Nearest Railway Station: Accrington (20min walk)
Parking (Car): Free places at ground located behind both goals; on-street parking in vicinity of ground
Parking (Coach/Bus): As directed
Other Clubs Sharing Ground: Burnley Reserves (tbc)
Police Force and Tel No: Lancashire Police (0845 125 3545)
Disabled Visitors' Facilities:
Wheelchairs: Available
Blind: No special facility

1 A680 Whalley Road
2 To town centre and
Accrington railway station
(one mile)
3 Livingstone Road
4 Cleveleys Road
5 Sophia Khan Stand
6 Coppice Terrace (away)

↑ North direction (approx)

◄ 701911
▼ 701918

aldershot town

The EBB Stadium at The Recreation Ground, High Street, Aldershot, Hampshire GU11 1TW

website: **WWW.THE SHOTS.CO.UK**
e:mail: **ENQUIRIES@THESHOTS.CO.UK**
tel no: **01252 320211**
colours: **RED SHIRTS WITH BLUE TRIM, RED SHORTS**
nickname: **THE SHOTS**
season 2010/11: **LEAGUE TWO**

Last Season: **6th** (p**46**; w**20**; d**12**; l**14**; gf**69**; ga**56**)

After 30 months in the managerial role at Aldershot and having guided the club both back into the Football League and ensuring its survival in League Two, Gary Waddock departed in mid-October to take over at Wycombe Wanderers. He was succeeded as caretaker boss by Jason Dodd; however, Dodd's role was to be short-lived as he left in early November to become the head of Southampton's academy. The club moved quickly to appoint ex-Reading coach Kevin Dillon to the vacancy. He inherited a club that was in the pack chasing the Play-Off places and, under his management, a top-seven position was secured following the 3-1 home win over Lincoln City in the penultimate League match of the season. Unfortunately, however, defeats both home and away against Rotherham United mean that the Shots will again be playing in League Two in 2010/11 but the team should once again feature in the battle for the Play-Offs at least.

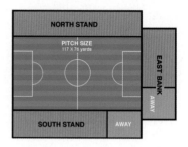

Advance Tickets Tel No: 01252 320211
Fax: 01252 324347
Training Ground: Address withheld as it's located on MoD property
Brief History: Aldershot FC established in 1926 and played its first game at the Recreation Ground in 1927. Elected to the Football League (Third Division [South]) for the start of the 1932/33 season. Club failed to complete the 1991/92 season and lost its League membership. A new club, Aldershot Town, was established and, having progressed up the non-league pyramid, won promotion back to the Football League at the end of the 2007/08 season. Record attendance: (as Aldershot) 19,138; (as Aldershot Town) 7,500.
(Total) Current Capacity: 7,100 (1,885 seated)
Visiting Supporters' Allocation: c1,100 (212 seated) in the South Stand and East Bank.
Nearest Railway Station: Aldershot
Parking (Car): Pay & display car parks in the town centre
Parking (Coach/Bus): As directed
Other Clubs Sharing Ground: Reading Reserves
Police Force and Tel No: Hampshire (01962 841534)
Disabled Visitors' Facilities:
Wheelchairs: 10 spaces High Street End
Blind: No special facility

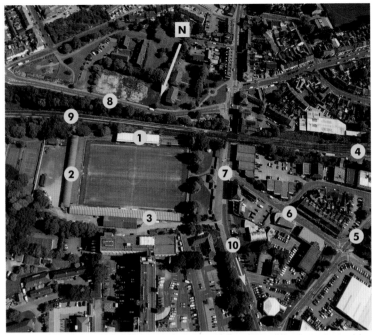

1 South Stand
2 East Bank
3 North Stand
4 Aldershot railway station
5 Windsor Way
6 Victoria Road
7 A323 High Street
8 Redan Road
9 Railway line towards Woking and London
10 A323 towards Fleet

↑ *North direction (approx)*

◄ 701172
▼ 701171

arsenal

Emirates Stadium, Highbury House, 75 Drayton Park, London N5 1BU

website: **WWW.ARSENAL.COM**
e:mail: **CONTACT VIA WEBSITE**
tel no: **020 7619 5003**
colours: **RED AND WHITE SHIRTS, WHITE SHORTS**
nickname: **THE GUNNERS**
season 2010/11: **PREMIER LEAGUE**

Last Season: **3rd** (p**38**; w**23**; d**6**; l**9**; gf**83**; ga**41**)

It's now five years since the Gunners last won a trophy – the FA Cup at the end of the 2004/05 season – and whilst Arsene Wenger's teams have been widely praised for the quality of the football that they have produced – much of which was undeniably sublime at times – the continuing failure to deliver silverware will be a cause of concern. Undoubtedly the team has suffered perhaps more than its fair share of injuries – with Arshavin, Fabregas, van Persie, Ramsey and others all succumbing at various stages during the season – but more critical was perhaps the failure to replace Adebayor as a main striker and suspicions that the team lacks a true world-class keeper. With competing teams looking to the transfer market to bolster their squads, if Arsenal are to be serious candidates for the title then Wenger may need to dip into the war-chest that seems likely to be available to him. Without a doubt, Arsenal will continue to be serious challengers for the title in 2010/11 but their ability to sustain it through to the end of the campaign will depend on how the squad is improved over the summer. As in previous years, the club's best opportunity for silverware may well again come in the cup competitions.

Advance Tickets Tel No: 020 7619 5000
Fax: 020 7704 4001
Training Ground: Bell Lane, London Colney, St Albans AL2 1DR
Brief History: Founded 1886 as Royal Arsenal, changed to Woolwich Arsenal in 1891 and Arsenal in 1914. Former grounds: Plumstead Common, Sportsman Ground, Manor Ground (twice), moved to Arsenal Stadium in 1913 and to new Emirates Stadium for start of the 2006/07 season. Record attendance (at Highbury) 73,295; 60,161 (at Emirates Stadium).
(Total) Current Capacity: 60,432
Visiting Supporters' Allocation: 3,000 (South East Corner)
Nearest Railway Station: Finsbury Park or Drayton Park (Network Rail); Arsenal and Holloway Road (Underground)
Parking (Car): Residents' only parking scheme with special permits in the streets surrounding the ground and local road closures on matchdays
Parking (Coach/Bus): Queensland Road and Sobell Centre car park or as directed by the police
Police Force and Tel No: Metropolitan (0300 123 1212)
Disabled Visitors' Facilities:
Wheelchairs: c250 places around the ground
Blind: 98 seats available but over subscribed

▲ 703298
◄ 703296

1 North Bridge
2 South Bridge
3 Drayton Park station
4 Drayton Park
5 East Coast Main Line
6 To Finsbury Park station
7 Arsenal Underground station
8 South East Corner (away)

↑ North direction (approx)

aston villa

Villa Park, Trinity Road, Birmingham, B6 6HE

website: **WWW.AVFC.PREMIUMTV.CO.UK**
e:mail: **POSTMASTER@AVFC.CO.UK**
tel no: **0121 327 2299**
colours: **CLARET AND BLUE SHIRTS, WHITE SHORTS**
nickname: **THE VILLANS**
season 2010/11: **PREMIER LEAGUE**

Last Season: **6th** (p**38**; w**17**; d**13**; l**8**; gf**52**; ga **39**)

Ultimately, whilst finishing in sixth place again ensures European football courtesy of the Europa League at Villa Park, the last season was perhaps again one of missed opportunities for Martin O'Neill and his Villa team. Although, despite some uncertainty, O'Neill will still be manager for the new campaign, he's been given a reduced budget to work with and it's difficult to predict what impact this will have on his ability to add that element of quality to a talented squad to give it that little bit extra. In the League, Villa had the opportunity of making a sustained challenge for a top-four position – given Liverpool's obvious frailty – but never seemed to be in the hunt as seriously as Tottenham and Manchester City. The European adventure ended early following defeat by Rapid Vienna on the away goals rule, but the Carling Cup proved much more successful, with the team reaching the Wembley final. However, despite taking an early lead through James Milner, Villa were ultimately to suffer a 2-1 defeat at the hands of Manchester United. In the FA Cup, Villa again prospered before being beaten 3-0 by Chelsea in the semi-final at Wembley; it might, however, have been a different story if the strong first-half shout for a Villa penalty had been given by referee Howard Webb. For the new season, Villa should again be one of the teams vying for a place in the Europa League spots but it's hard to see the team making that break and getting into the top four. As in 2009/10, the club's best route to silverware may well be again through one of the cup competitions.

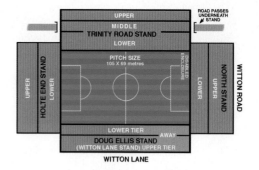

Advance Tickets Tel No: 0800 612 0970
Fax: 0121 322 2107
Training Ground: Bodymoor Heath Lane, Middleton, Tamworth B78 2BB
Brief History: Founded in 1874. Founder Members Football League (1888). Former Grounds: Aston Park and Lower Aston Grounds and Perry Barr, moved to Villa Park (a development of the Lower Aston Grounds) in 1897. Record attendance 76,588
(Total) Current Capacity: 42,640 (all seated)
Visiting Supporters' Allocation: Approx 3,000 in Doug Ellis Stand
Nearest Railway Station: Witton
Parking (Car): Asda car park, Aston Hall Road
Parking (Coach/Bus): Asda car park, Aston Hall Road (special coach park for visiting supporters situated in Witton Lane)
Police Force and Tel No: West Midlands (0345 113 5000)
Disabled Visitors' Facilities:
Wheelchairs: Trinity Road Stand section
Blind: Commentary by arrangement
Anticipated Development(s): In order to increase the ground's capacity to 51,000 Planning Permission has been obtained to extend the North Stand with two corner in-fills. There is, however, no confirmed timescale for the work to be completed.

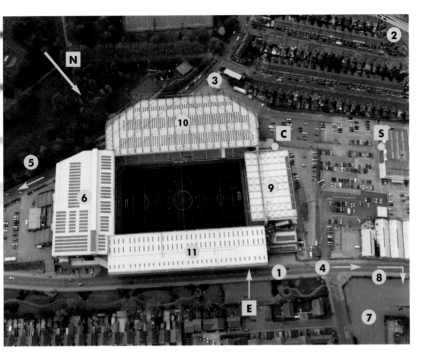

C Club Offices
S Club Shop
E Entrance(s) for visiting supporters

1 B4137 Witton Lane
2 B4140 Witton Road
3 Trinity Road
4 To A4040 Aston Lane to A34 Walsall Road
5 To Aston Expressway & M6
6 Holte End
7 Visitors' Car Park
8 To Witton railway station
9 North Stand
10 Trinity Road Stand
11 Doug Ellis Stand

⬆ North direction (approx)

◄ 701001
▾ 701003

barnet

Underhill Stadium, Barnet Lane, Barnet, Herts EN5 2DN

website: **WWW.BARNETFC.COM**
e:mail: **INFO@BARNETFC.COM**
tel no: **020 8441 6932**
colours: **BLACK/GOLD SHIRTS, BLACK SHORTS**
nickname: **THE BEES**
season 2010/11: **LEAGUE TWO**

Last Season: **21st** (p**46**; w**12**; d**12**; l**22**; gf**47**; ga**63**)

At the end of April, following a run of four wins and four draws out of the 22 League games played in 2010 that left Barnet in 22nd place having briefly led League Two in September, Ian Hendon was sacked as manager after only a year in charge. He was replaced as caretaker boss by ex-manager Paul Fairclough, whose first game in charge was, ironically, away at Grimsby Town – the team at that stage lying in 23rd place and capable of escaping relegation at Barnet's expense if results went against the Bees. A 2-0 home victory meant that Barnet's fate would not be decided until the final Saturday of the season when a home fixture against already promoted Rochdale was on offer whilst Grimsby faced a difficult away match at Burton Albion. Also threatened were Cheltenham Town at home to an Accrington side in freefall down the table. In the event, home victory for Barnet combined with Cheltenham's draw was enough to consign Grimsby to relegation irrespective of the result at the Pirelli Stadium (Grimsby, in fact, lost 3-0 and went down amidst some crowd scenes). Although Barnet are safe for another season under new manager Mark Stimson (appointed in early July), it again looks as though the club will struggle to retain its League status come May 2011.

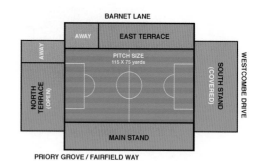

Advance Tickets Tel No: 020 8449 6325

Fax: 020 8447 0655

Brief History: Founded 1888 as Barnet Alston. Changed name to Barnet (1919). Former grounds: Queens Road and Totteridge Lane; moved to Underhill in 1906. Promoted to Football League 1991; relegated to Conference 2001; promoted to League 2 2005. Record attendance, 11,026

(Total) Current Capacity 5,500

Visiting Supporters' Allocation: 1,000 on East Terrace (open) plus 500 on North Terrace is required.

Nearest Railway Station: New Barnet (High Barnet – Tube)

Parking (Car): Street Parking and High Barnet station

Parking (Coach/Bus): As directed by police

Other Clubs sharing ground: Arsenal Reserves

Police Force and Tel No: Metropolitan (0300 123 1212)

Anticipated Development(s): Following the granting of Planning Permission, the club opened its new £500,000 1,000 seat South Stand on 22 January 2008. The 200 seats from the uncovered temporary stand have been relocated under cover at the northeast side of the ground for use by away fans.

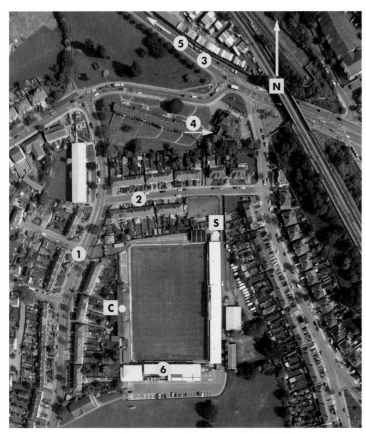

C Club Offices
S Club Shop

1 Barnet Lane
2 Westcombe Drive
3 A1000 Barnet Hill
4 New Barnet railway station
   (one mile)
5 To High Barnet tube station,
   M1 and M25
6 South Stand

↑ North direction (approx)

◄ 701191
▼ 701197

barnsley

Oakwell Stadium, Grove Street, Barnsley, S71 1ET

website: **WWW.BARNSLEYFC.CO.UK**
e:mail: **THEREDS@BARNSLEYFC.CO.UK**
tel no: **01226 211211**
colours: **RED SHIRTS, WHITE SHORTS**
nickname: **THE TYKES**
season 2010/11: **CHAMPIONSHIP**

Last Season: **18th** (p**46**; w**14**; d**12**; l**20**; gf**53**; ga**69**)

After two-and-a-half years at Oakwell, Simon Davey became the first managerial casualty in the Championship when, following a 3-1 home defeat by Reading – a result that left the Tykes rock bottom of the division with a single point from their first five League matches – he left the club at the end of August. The club moved quickly to appoint Mark Robins, who'd proved a considerable success at Rotherham under difficult circumstances, to the Oakwell hot-seat. Under Robins' guidance, the club managed a 3-2 home victory against Premier League strugglers Burnley in the 3rd round of the Carling Cup and also progressed up the Championship table to the point where the Play-Offs were a serious possibility in early February. A late loss of form, however, that saw the team win only three of its last 18 League matches, with no victory at all in the final 10, resulted in an inexorable slip down the table. Having garnered enough points earlier in the season there was little likelihood that relegation would result from this late loss of form but fans will be worried confidence will be low and that, without judicious strengthening, the squad could again struggle in 2010/11. A position of mid-table safety is perhaps the best that fans can look forward to.

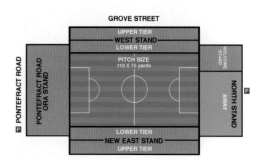

Advance Tickets Tel No: 0871 226 6777

Fax: 01226 211444

Training Ground: Adjacent to ground

Brief History: Founded in 1887 as Barnsley St Peter's, changed name to Barnsley in 1897. Former Ground: Doncaster Road, Worsboro Bridge until 1888. Record attendance 40,255

(Total) Current Capacity: 23,009 (all seated)

Visiting Supporters' Allocation: 6,000 maximum (all seated; North Stand)

Nearest Railway Station: Barnsley

Parking (Car): Queen's Ground car park

Parking (Coach/Bus): Queen's Ground car park

Police Force and Tel No: South Yorkshire (0114 220 2020)

Disabled Visitors' Facilities:

Wheelchairs: Purpose built disabled stand

Blind: Commentary available

Future Development(s): With the completion of the new North Stand with its 6,000 capacity, the next phase for the redevelopment of Oakwell will feature the old West Stand with its remaining open seating. There is, however, no timescale for this work.

C Club Offices
S Club Shop
E Entrance(s) for visiting
supporters

1 A628 Pontefract Road
2 To Barnsley Exchange railway
station and M1 Junction 37
(two miles)
3 Queen's Ground Car Park
4 North Stand
5 Grove Street
6 To Town Centre

⬆ North direction (approx)

◀ 701015
▾ 701021

birmingham city

St Andrew's Stadium, St Andrew's Street, Birmingham B9 4RL

website: **WWW.BCFC.COM**
e:mail: **RECEPTION@BCFC.COM**
tel no: **0844 557 1875**
colours: **BLUE AND WHITE SHIRTS, WHITE SHORTS**
nickname: **THE BLUES**
season 2010/11: **PREMIER LEAGUE**

Last Season: **9th** (p**38**; w**13**; d**11**; l**14**; gf**38**; ga**47**)

Promoted at the end of the 2008/09 season, the first priority for Alex McLeish's team was always going to be survival in the Premier League and after a steady start to the season, a run of 15 League and Cup matches from late October through to late January saw the team unbeaten. At this stage of the season, the team was within shouting distance of an unlikely place in Europe as it vied for a top-six place. For fans, however, more worrying will be the late slump in form, with City winning only one of the team's last 10 League matches. A haul of only seven points from those matches is more relegation form than Europa League material and McLeish will need to make some significant improvements to the squad if a relegation battle isn't to ensue in 2010/11. Much of the club's stability in 2009/10 was the result of bringing in Manchester City keeper Joe Hart in on loan; with Hart returning to his parent club, McLeish moved swiftly to bring in ex-Manchester United keeper Ben Foster as replacement. One suspects that he'll need to do more if City are to replicate their best League finish for more than 50 years.

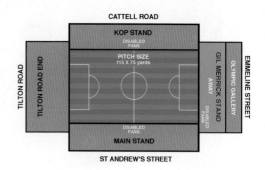

Advance Tickets Tel No: 0844 557 1875
Fax: 0844 557 1975
Training Ground: Wast Hills, Redhill Road, Kings Norton, Birmingham B38 9EJ. 0121 244 1401
Brief History: Founded 1875, as Small Heath Alliance. Changed to Small Heath in 1888, Birmingham in 1905, Birmingham City in 1945. Former Grounds: Arthur Street, Ladypool Road, Muntz Street, moved to St Andrew's in 1906. Record attendance 66,844
(Total) Current Capacity: 30,016 (all seated)
Visiting Supporters' Allocation: 3-4,500 in new Railway End (Lower Tier)
Nearest Railway Station: Bordesley
Parking (Car): Street parking
Parking (Coach/Bus): Coventry Road
Police Force and Tel No: West Midlands (0345 113 5000)
Disabled Visitors' Facilities:
Wheelchairs: 90 places; advanced notice required
Blind: Commentary available
Future Development(s): The proposals for the Digbeth ground have not progressed and any future development is likely to involve work at St Andrew's, where there are plans for the possible redevelopment of the Main Stand to take the ground's capacity to 36,500. There is no timescale for the £12 million project.

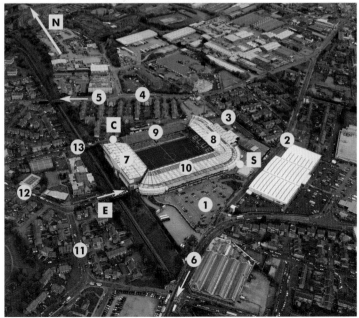

▲ 701032
◄ 701034

C Club Offices
S Club Shop
E Entrance(s) for visiting
   supporters

1 Car Park
2 B4128 Cattell Road
3 Tilton Road
4 Garrison Lane
5 To A4540 & A38 (M)
6 To City Centre and
   New Street railway Station
   (1½ miles)
7 Gil Merrick (Railway End)
   Stand
8 Tilton Road End
9 Main Stand
10 Kop Stand
11 Emmeline Street
12 Kingston Road
13 St Andrew's Street

⬆ *North direction (approx)*

blackburn rovers

Ewood Park, Blackburn, Lancashire, BB2 4JF

website: **WWW.ROVERS.CO.UK**
e:mail: **COMMERCIAL@ROVERS.CO.UK**
tel no: **0871 702 1875**
colours: **BLUE AND WHITE HALVED SHIRTS, WHITE SHORTS**
nickname: **ROVERS**
season 2010/11: **PREMIER LEAGUE**

Last Season: **10th** (p**38**; w**13**; d**11**;l**14**; gf**41**; ga**55**)

Under the pragmatic Sam Allardyce, in his first full season in charge at Ewood Park, Blackburn Rovers proved to be one of those Premier League teams that were never too good seriously to threaten the top places but conversely never too poor to be dragged into the relegation fight. Away from the League, the club had an impressive run in the Carling Cup, defeating Chelsea at home on penalties, before succumbing to eventual finalists Aston Villa. Rovers fans must have hated Villa during the season as the same team also dumped them out of the FA Cup in the 3rd Round. The club's late season form – with only one defeat in the final nine League matches – plus the likelihood that Allardyce will again be able both to retain key players and make judicious signings, mean that Rovers' fans can again look perhaps towards chasing a place in the Europa League in 2010/11.

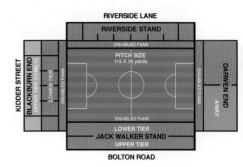

Advance Tickets Tel No: 0871 222 1444
Fax: 01254 671042
Training Ground: Brockhall Training Ground, The Avenue, Brockhall Village, Blackburn BB6 8AW
Brief History: Founded 1875. Former Grounds: Oozebooth, Pleasington Cricket Ground, Alexandra Meadows. Moved to Ewood Park in 1890. Founder members of Football League (1888).
Record attendance 61,783
(Total) Current Capacity: 31,367
Visiting Supporters' Allocation: 3,914 at the Darwen End
Nearest Railway Station: Blackburn
Parking (Car): Street parking and c800 spaces at ground
Parking (Coach/Bus): As directed by Police
Police Force and Tel No: Lancashire (0845 125 3545)
Disabled Visitors' Facilities:
Wheelchairs: All sides of the ground
Blind: Commentary available
Anticipated Development(s): There remain plans to redevelop the Riverside Stand to take Ewood Park's capacity to c40,000, but there is no confirmation as to if and when this work will be undertaken.

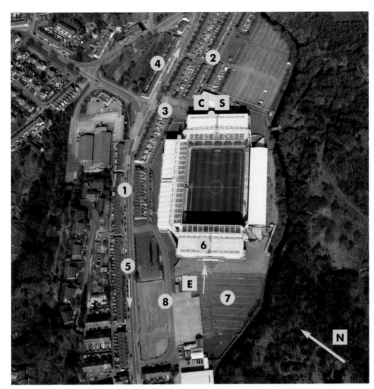

C Club Offices
S Club Shop
E Entrance(s) for visiting
   supporters

1 A666 Bolton Road
2 Kidder Street
3 Nuttall Street
4 Town Centre & Blackburn
   Central railway station
   (1 1/2 miles)
5 To Darwen and Bolton
6 Darwen End
7 Car Parks
8 Top O'Croft Road

↑ North direction (approx)

◄ 701879
▼ 701888

blackpool

Bloomfield Road, Seasiders Way, Blackpool FY1 6JJ

website: **WWW.BLACKPOOLFC.CO.UK**
e:mail: **INFO@BLACKPOOLFC.CO.UK**
tel no: **0871 622 1953**
colours: **TANGERINE SHIRTS, WHITE SHORTS**
nickname: **THE SEASIDERS**
season 2010/11: **PREMIER LEAGUE**

Last Season: **6th** (promoted) (p**46**; w**19**; d**13**;l**14**; gf **74**; ga**58**)

Widely seen as relegation fodder at the start of the season, Ian Holloway's Blackpool outfit proved to be one of the surprise packages in the Championship in 2009/10. A slow start to the League season with four draws in the first four fixtures seemed to indicate a season of toil, but the 4-1 home victory over Premier League Wigan in the 2nd Round of the Carling cup showed the team's potential and from then on the club seemed to be in the hunt – albeit for much of the season on the fringe – for a Play-Off place. It was not, however, until the final Sunday of the season that the club's fate was determined. Needing to match or better Swansea City's result at home to Doncaster Rovers, Blackpool's 1-1 draw with Bristol City was enough to see the Seasiders squeeze into the Play-Offs. Victories home and away over Nottingham Forest took Holloway's side to Wembley and a Final against Cardiff City. Despite going behind twice, three goals culminating in Brett Ormerod's winner just before half-time was sufficient to see the team victorious and thus restore Blackpool to the top flight for the first time in some 40 years. With the smallest ground in the Premier League by some margin, Blackpool will undoubtedly struggle to survive at this level. The heart would like to suggest that Blackpool could; the head, however, suggests that the team may well struggle to match Stoke City's tally for the lowest number of points achieved in the Premier League.

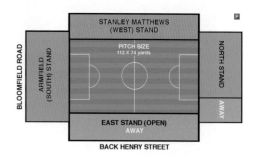

Advance Tickets Tel No: 0871 622 1953
Fax: 01253 405011
Training Ground: Squires Gate Training Ground, Martin Avenue, Lytham St Annes FY8 2SJ
Brief History: Founded 1887, merged with 'South Shore' (1899). Former grounds: Raikes Hall (twice) and Athletic Grounds, Stanley Park, South Shore played at Cow Cap Lane, moved to Bloomfield Road in 1899. Record attendance 38,098
(Total) Current Capacity: 13,500 (all seated)
Visiting Supporters' Allocation: 1,600 in North Stand plus 1,750 in East Stand if required (and before redevelopment)
Nearest Railway Station: Blackpool South
Parking (Car): At Ground and street parking (also behind West Stand – from M55)
Parking (Coach/Bus): Mecca car park (behind North End (also behind West Stand – from M55)
Other Club Sharing Ground: Blackpool Panthers RLFC
Police Force and Tel No: Lancashire (0845 125 3545)
Disabled Visitors' Facilities:
Wheelchairs: North and West stands
Blind: Commentary available (limited numbers)
Anticipated Development(s): Work on the construction of the new 3,600-seat South Stand was started in the summer of 2009. The £8.5 million structure was completed in December 2009 and was named after Jimmy Armfield. Following promotion to the Premier League the club has announced its intention to complete Bloomfield Road with construction of a new East Stand, for which planning consent already exists, to start as soon as possible. Once completed, the ground will have a capacity of 16,000.

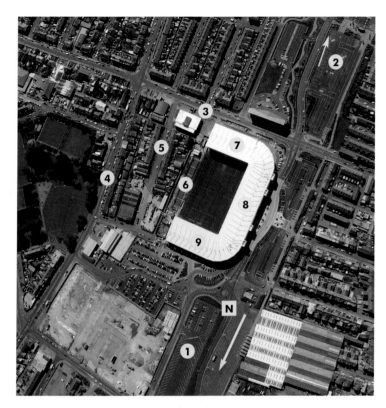

1 Car Park
2 To Blackpool South railway
   station (1½ miles) and
   M55 Junction 4
3 Bloomfield Road
4 A5099 Central Drive
5 Henry Street
6 East Stand (away)
   (being rebuilt)
7 South Stand
8 West (Pricebusters Matthews)
   Stand
9 North Stand

↑ North direction (approx)

◄ 703128
▼ 703139

bolton wanderers

Reebok Stadium, Burnden Way, Lostock, Bolton BL6 6JW

website: **WWW.BWFC.CO.UK**
e:mail: **RECEPTION@BWFC.CO.UK**
tel no: **0844 871 2932**
colours: **WHITE SHIRTS, WHITE SHORTS**
nickname: **THE TROTTERS**
season 2010/11: **PREMIER LEAGUE**

Last Season: **14th** (p**38**; w**10**; d**9**; l**19**; gf**42**; ga**67**)

Never wholly popular at the Reebok Stadium, Gary Megson's reign as Bolton Wanderers' manager came to an end shortly after Christmas following the 2-2 home draw against Hull City, a result that left Wanderers in 18th position and facing their annual battle to avoid the drop. Megson had been in charge at the club for two years and had secured the club's Premier League survival at the end of both the 2007/08 and 2008/09 seasons although having a somewhat fractious relationship with some elements of the home fans. The club moved quickly to appoint Owen Coyle, who'd brought Burnley up at the end of the 2008/09 season, to the vacancy. Coyle's controversial move saw him curry little favour with the fans at his erstwhile club as he commented that he believed that Wanderers had a better chance of surviving in the Premier League and in this he was proved right, although it was not until the 2-2 home draw with already relegated Portsmouth that the club was mathematically safe from the drop. Coyle proved at Burnley that he could achieve much with limited resources and, although his experience at this level is still limited, he ought to be able to ensure that Bolton survive another season in the top flight.

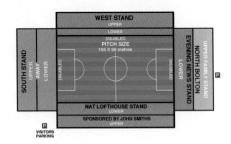

Advance Tickets Tel No: 0844 871 2932
Fax: 01204 673 773
Training Ground: Euxton Training Ground, Euxton Lane, Chorley PR7 6FA
Brief History: Founded 1874 as Christ Church; name changed 1877. Former grounds: Several Fields, Pikes Lane (1880-95) and Burnden Park (1895-1997). Moved to Reebok Stadium for 1997/98 season. Record attendance (Burnden Park): 69,912. Record attendance of 28,353 at Reebok Stadium

(Total) Current Capacity: 28,723 (all seated)
Visiting Supporters' Allocation: 5,000 maximum (South Stand)
Club Colours: White shirts, white shorts
Nearest Railway Station: Horwich Parkway
Parking (Car): 2,800 places at ground with up to 3,000 others in proximity
Parking (Coach/Bus): As directed
Police Force and Tel No: Greater Manchester (0161 872 5050)
Disabled Visitors' Facilities:
Wheelchairs: c100 places around the ground
Blind: Commentary available

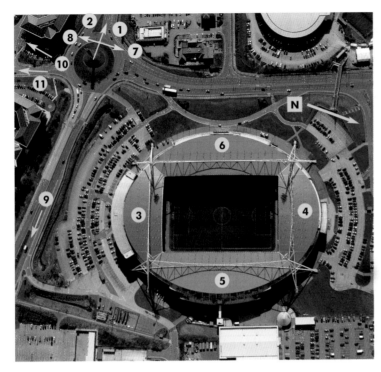

1 To Junction 6 of M61
2 A6027 Horwich link road
3 South Stand (away)
4 North Stand
5 Nat Lofthouse Stand
6 West Stand
7 M61 northbound to M6 and Preston (at J6)
8 M61 southbound to Manchester (at J6)
9 To Horwich and Bolton
10 To Lostock Junction station
11 To Horwich Parkway station

↑ North direction (approx)

◄ 700989
▼ 700996

afc bournemouth

Dean Court, Kings Park, Bournemouth, Dorset, BH7 7AF

website: **WWW.AFCB.CO.UK**
e:mail: **ENQUIRIES@AFCB.CO.UK**
tel no: **01202 726300**
colours: **RED AND BLACK SHIRTS, BLACK SHORTS**
nickname: **THE CHERRIES**
season 2010/11: **LEAGUE ONE**

Last Season: **2nd** (promoted) (p**46**; w**25**; d**8**; l**13**; gf**61**; ga**44**;)

Although starting the 2008/09 season with the disadvantage of a 17-deduction as a result of going into Administration, Bournemouth's form in the second half of the season, following the appointment of Eddie Howe, then the youngest manager in the Football League, as manager indicated that the Cherries might be a force come 2009/10. In the hunt for automatic promotion and the Play-Offs for virtually all the season, promotion back to League One was confirmed towards the end of April following the 1-0 victory away at Burton United. Fans and the manager will, however, be fully aware that winning promotion is but half the battle; retaining League One status will be equally if not more difficult. It's hard to escape the conclusion that, with the club's financial position, a battle against the drop by May 2011 may be hard to win.

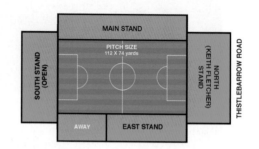

Advance Tickets Tel No: 01202 726338
Fax: 01202 726373
Training Ground: Canford School, Court House, Canford Magna, Wimborne BH21 3AF
Brief History: Founded 1890 as Boscombe St. John's, changed to Boscombe (1899), Bournemouth & Boscombe Athletic (1923) and A.F.C. Bournemouth (1971). Former grounds Kings Park (twice) and Castlemain Road, Pokesdown. Moved to Dean Court in 1910.
Record attendance 28,799; since rebuilding: 10,375

(Total) Current Capacity: 10,375 (all seated)
Visiting Supporters' Allocation: 1,500 in East Stand (can be increased to 2,000 if required)
Nearest Railway Station: Bournemouth
Parking (Car): Large car park adjacent ground
Parking (Coach/Bus): Large car park adjacent ground
Police Force and Tel No: Dorset (01202 222222)
Disabled Visitors' Facilities:
Wheelchairs: 100 spaces
Blind: No special facility
Anticipated Development(s): The club still intends to construct a South Stand at Dean Court, taking the ground's capacity to just under 12,000 but there is no confirmed schedule.

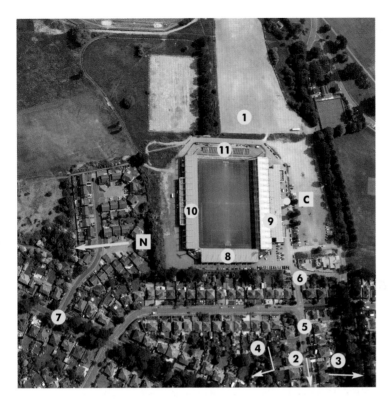

C Club Offices

1 Car Park
2 A338 Wessex Way
3 To Bournemouth Station
 (1½ miles)
4 To A31 & M27
5 Thistlebarrow Road
6 King's Park Drive
7 Littledown Avenue
8 North (Keith Fletcher) Stand
9 Main Stand
10 East Stand
11 Site of proposed South Stand

↑ *North direction (approx)*

◄ 701244
▼ 701253

bradford city

Coral Windows Stadium, Valley Parade, Bradford, BD8 7DY

website: **WWW.BRADFORDCITYFC.CO.UK**
e:mail: **BRADFORDCITYFC@COMPUSERVE.COM**
tel no: **01274 773355**
colours: **AMBER SHIRTS, CLARET SHORTS**
nickname: **THE BANTAMS**
season 2010/11: **LEAGUE TWO**

Last Season: **14th** (p**46**; w**16**; d**14**; l**16**; gf**59**; ga**62**)

Again widely considered as one of the pre-season favourites for promotion and with City legend Stuart McCall still in the managerial seat, hopes were high that the club would end its three-year sojourn in League Two. The reality was, however, that the team struggled to make an impact and following a 1-0 reverse at Valley Parade, a result that left the Bantams in 16th place, McCall stood down as manager in mid-February. Following a single match with first-team coach Wayne Jacobs in charge, the club moved quickly to bring in the experienced Peter Taylor as boss. The new manager started the process of revising the squad, releasing a number of players and bringing a number of loanees in. Under Taylor, the Bantams' performance improved, although never really being able to overturn the 12-point gap to seventh place that he inherited. However, Taylor's arrival and the form of the team in the latter part of the season will encourage City fans in the belief that 2010/11 really will be their team's turn to achieve promotion.

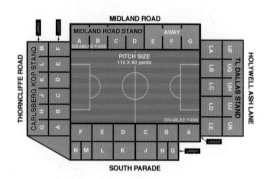

Advance Tickets Tel No: 01274 770012
Fax: 01274 773356
Training Ground: Rawdon Meadows, Apperley Bridge, Bradford
Brief History: Founded 1903 (formerly Manningham Northern Union Rugby Club founded in 1876). Continued use of Valley Parade, joined 2nd Division on re-formation. Record attendance: 39,146
(Total) Current Capacity: 25,136 (All seated)
Visiting Supporters' Allocation: 1,300-1,800 (all seated) in Midland Stand
Nearest Railway Station: Bradford Forster Square
Parking (Car): Street parking and car parks
Parking (Coach/Bus): As directed by Police
Police Force and Tel No: West Yorkshire (0845 600 0600)
Disabled Visitors' Facilities:
Wheelchairs: 110 places in Co-Operative, Midland Road and Carlsberg stands
Blind: Commentary available
Anticipated Development(s): With work on the Main (Co-Operative) Stand now completed, Valley Parade has a slightly unbalanced look. The club has proposals for the reconstruction of the Midland Road Stand to take the ground's capacity to 30,000, although, given the club's current League position, there is no time-scale.

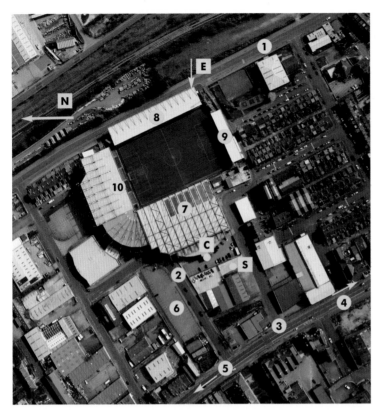

C Club Offices
S Club Shop
E Entrance(s) for visiting
   supporters

1 Midland Road
2 Valley Parade
3 A650 Manningham Lane
4 To City Centre, Forster
   Square and Interchange
   stations M606 & M62
5 To Keighley
6 Car Parks
7 Co-Operative Stand
8 Midland Road Stand
9 TL Dallas Stand
10 Carlsberg Kop Stand

↑ North direction (approx)

◀ 701968
▾ 701086

brentford

Griffin Park, Braemar Road, Brentford, Middlesex, TW8 0NT

website: **WWW.BRENTFORDFC.CO.UK**
e:mail: **ENQUIRIES@BRENTFORDFC.CO.UK**
tel no: **0845 3456 442**
colours: **RED AND WHITE STRIPES, BLACK SHORTS**
nickname: **THE BEES**
season 2010/11: **LEAGUE ONE**

Last Season: **9th** (p**46**; w**14**; d**20**; l**12**; gf**55**; ga**52**)

Coming up as champions from League Two, Andy Scott's Brentford made a slow start to the season, winning only three of the team's first 13 League fixtures and failing to proceed beyond the 1st Round of the Carling Cup. Thereafter the team's form picked up and the club moved steadily up the League One table. In the event, however, the relatively poor start to the season meant that the team was always playing catch-up and so ultimately finishing in ninth place – albeit 18 points off the all-important sixth place – was better than appeared possible earlier in the season. Provided that the on-field progress can be maintained into 2010/11, it's possible that Brentford may make a more sustained push for the Play-Offs at least in the new campaign.

Advance Tickets Tel No: 0845 3456 442

Fax: 020 8568 9940

Training Ground: Osterley Training Ground, 100 Jersey Road, Hounslow TW5 0TP

Brief History: Founded 1889. Former Grounds: Clifden House Ground, Benn's Field (Little Ealing), Shotters Field, Cross Roads, Boston Park Cricket Ground, moved to Griffin Park in 1904. Founder-members Third Division (1920). Record attendance 38,678

(Total) Current Capacity: 12,763 (8,905 seated)

Visiting Supporters' Allocation: 1,600 in Brook Road Stand (600 seated)

Nearest Railway Station: Brentford, South Ealing (tube)

Parking (Car): Street parking (restricted)

Parking (Coach/Bus): Layton Road car park

Other Club Sharing Ground: Chelsea Reserves

Police Force and Tel No: Metropolitan (0300 123 1212)

Disabled Visitors' Facilities:

Wheelchairs: Braemar Road

Blind: Commentary available

Anticipated Development(s): Although the club still intends to relocate, a roof was installed over the Ealing Road Terrace in 2007 with home fans being transferred to that end. With a view to relocation, a site on Lionel Road has been identified although there is no confirmed timetable as to when or if work will commence.

C Club Offices
S Club Shop
E Entrance(s) for visiting
supporters

1 Ealing Road
2 Braemar Road
3 Brook Road South
4 To M4 ($^1/_4$ mile) & South
Ealing Tube Station
(1 mile)
5 Brentford station
6 To A315 High Street
& Kew Bridge
7 New Road
8 Ealing Road Terrace
9 Brook Road Stand (away)

↑ *North direction (approx)*

◄ 701308
▼ 701306

brighton and hove albion

Withdean Stadium, Tongdean Lane, Brighton, BN1 5JD

club office: **8th FLOOR, TOWER POINT, 44 NORTH ROAD, BRIGHTON BN1 1YR**
website: **WWW.SEAGULLS.CO.UK**
e:mail: **SEAGULLS@BHAFC.CO.UK**
tel no: **01273 695400**
colours: **BLUE AND WHITE STRIPED SHIRTS, WHITE SHORTS**
nickname: **THE SEAGULLS**
season 2010/11: **LEAGUE ONE**

Last Season: **13th** (p**46**; w**15**; d**14**; l**17**; gf**56**; ga**60**)

At the start of November, following a 3-3 draw with Hartlepool (a result that left the Seagulls just above the League One drop zone), Russell Slade was sacked as Brighton manager after only eight months in the job. Within a few days the club appointed the former Spurs and Leeds assistant manager, Gus Poyet, to the vacancy and under the new manager the club's form picked up. Winning 12 and drawing nine of the last 31 matches of the season brought the Seagulls up to a position of some mid-table respectability. Provided that the form shown in the latter part of the 2009/10 season is replicated come the new season, then Poyet's team should have the potential to get into the top half of the table and perhaps threaten a Play-Off place.

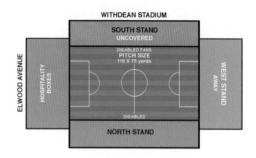

WITHDEAN STADIUM

SOUTH STAND
UNCOVERED

DISABLED FANS
PITCH SIZE
110 X 75 yards

ELWOOD AVENUE

HOSPITALITY BOXES

WEST STAND AWAY

DISABLED

NORTH STAND

Advance Ticket Tel No: 0845 496 1901
Fax: 01273 648179
Training Ground: University of Sussex, Falmer Sports Complex, Ridge Road, Falmer, Brighton BN1 9PL
Brief History: Founded 1900 as Brighton & Hove Rangers, changed to Brighton & Hove Albion 1902. Former grounds: Home Farm (Withdean), County Ground, Goldstone Ground (1902-1997), Priestfield Stadium (ground share with Gillingham) 1997-1999; moved to Withdean Stadium 1999. Founder members of the 3rd Division 1920. Record attendance (at Goldstone Ground): 36,747; at Withdean Stadium: 8,691.
(Total) Current Capacity: 8,850 (all seated)
Visiting Supporters' Allocation: 900 max on open West Stand
Nearest Railway Station: Preston Park
Parking (Cars): Street parking in the immediate vicinity of the ground is residents' only. This will be strictly enforced and it is suggested that intending visitors should use parking facilities away from the ground and use the proposed park and ride bus services that will be provided.
Parking (Coach/Bus): As directed
Police Force and Tel No: Sussex (0845 60 70 999)
Disabled Visitors' Facilities
Wheelchairs: Facilities in both North and South stands
Blind: No special facility
Anticipated Development(s): Work commenced on the construction of the new £60 million stadium at Falmer in the summer of 2009; if work goes according to schedule, the Seagulls should move to the new 22,373-seat facility for the start of the 2011/12 season. The club announced at the end of June 2010 that the new ground would be named the American Express Community Stadium.

▾ 702907

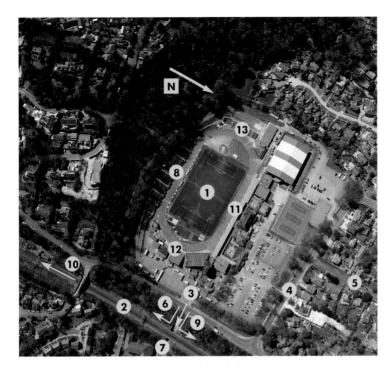

Shop Address:
6 Queen's Road, Brighton
Note: All games at Withdean will be
all-ticket with no cash
admissions on the day.

1 Withdean Stadium
2 London-Brighton railway line
3 To London Road (A23)
4 Tongdean Lane
5 Colebrook Road
6 To Brighton town centre
and main railway station
(1.75 miles)
7 Tongdean Lane (with bridge
under railway)
8 South Stand
9 A23 northwards to Crawley
10 To Preston Park railway station
11 North Stand
12 North East Stand
13 West Stand (away)

⬆ North direction (approx)

◄ 702914
▼ 702917

bristol city

Ashton Gate Stadium, Ashton Road, Bristol, BS3 2EJ

website: **WWW.BCFC.CO.UK**
e:mail: **ENQUIRIES@BCFC.CO.UK**
tel no: **0871 222 6666**
colours: **RED SHIRTS, WHITE SHORTS**
nickname: **THE ROBINS**
season 2010/11: **CHAMPIONSHIP**

Last Season: **10th** (p**46**; w**15**; d**18**; l**13**; gf**56**; ga**65**)

Following his success in taking Bristol City to the Play-Off Final at the end of 2008, the 2008/09 season had proved a disappointing campaign for Gary Johnson and the 2009/10 season was equally dismal. With the team in 15th place, only seven points above an increasingly competitive relegation zone and having only achieved two victories in the club's last 12 matches, Johnson departed from Ashton Gate in mid-March after more than four years at the helm. He was replaced, in a caretaker role, by his assistant Keith Millen before it was confirmed in mid-April that the experienced ex-Crystal Palace and Reading boss Steve Coppell was taking over as the new manager. Ultimately, the club was to finish in tenth place, seven points below the Play-Offs but the team's improved form towards the end of the season – with five wins and three draws in the final nine League matches – will make fans optimistic that, with the experienced Coppell in charge, a more sustained push for the Play-Offs at least can be maintained come the new season.

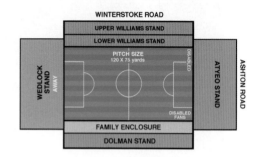

Tel No: 0117 963 0630
Advance Tickets Tel No: 0871 222 6666
Fax: 0117 963 0700
Training Ground: Queen Elizabeth Hospital's Playing Fields, Clevedon Road, Failand BS8 3TN
Brief History: Founded 1894 as Bristol South End changed to Bristol City in 1897. Former Ground: St John's Lane, Bedminster, moved to Ashton Gate in 1904. Record attendance 43,335
(Total) Current Capacity: 21,479 (all seated)
Visiting Supporters' Allocation: 3,000 in Wedlock Stand (all seated; can be increased to 5,500 if necessary)
Nearest Railway Station: Bristol Temple Meads
Parking (Car): Street parking
Parking (Coach/Bus): Marsh Road
Police Force and Tel No: Avon/Somerset (0845 456 7000)
Disabled Visitors' Facilities:
Wheelchairs: Limited
Blind: Commentary available
Anticipated Development(s): Plans for the £65 million ground at Ashton Vale were submitted to the Council in the summer of 2009. The initial scheme is for four stands with a seating capacity of 30,000 with the possibility of increasing this to 42,000 if necessary. In November 2009 the Council announced that it was minded to give approval to the scheme. In October 2009 the club revealed that Sainsbury, rather than Tesco, was now the preferred buyer for the Ashton Gate site. In early January 2010 it was announced that plans to include 120 houses alongside the stadium development had been dropped. The ground was selected as one of the 12 possible grounds for use in 2018 should England win the World Cup. If the bid proves successful, the ground's capacity would need to be raised to 44,000.

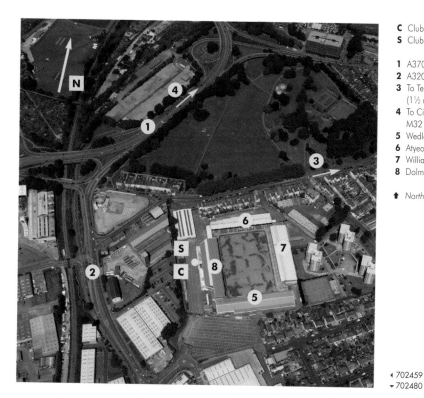

C Club Offices
S Club Shop

1 A370 Ashton Road
2 A3209 Winterstoke Road
3 To Temple Meads Station
  (1½ miles)
4 To City Centre, A4,
  M32 & M4
5 Wedlock Stand
6 Atyeo Stand
7 Williams Stand
8 Dolman Stand

↑ *North direction (approx)*

◀ 702459
▼ 702480

bristol rovers

The Memorial Stadium, Filton Avenue, Horfield, Bristol, BS7 0BF

website: **WWW.BRISTOLROVERS.CO.UK**
e:mail: **DAVE@BRISTOLROVERS.CO.UK**
tel no: **0117 909 6648**
colours: **BLUE AND WHITE QUARTERED SHIRTS, WHITE SHORTS**
nickname: **THE PIRATES (or Gasheads historically)**
season 2010/11: **LEAGUE ONE**

Last Season: **11th (p46; w19; d5; l22; gf59; ga70)**

A good start to the season saw Paul Trollope's team challenging for the automatic promotion spots at the end of September but this was to be the highpoint of the season as a subsequent run of six straight League defeats saw the team drift inexorably down the table. However, as late as late March the club was still in the hunt for the Play-offs. Unfortunately, however, even these slim hopes were dashed by a late drop in form, with the club only gaining four points from the last eight League matches. Granted two of the late defeats came against Norwich City and Leeds United – both of which ultimately achieved automatic promotion – but the failure to sustain the earlier challenge will be of concern to fans. For the new season, it looks again as if mid-table mediocrity ultimately beckons.

Advance Tickets Tel No: 0117 909 8848
Fax: 0117 907 4312
Training Ground: Bristol Academy of Sport, Filton College, Filton Avenue, Bristol BS34 7AT
Brief History: Founded 1883 as Black Arabs, changed to Eastville Rovers (1884), Bristol Eastville Rovers (1896) and Bristol Rovers (1897). Former grounds: Purdown, Three Acres, The Downs (Horfield), Ridgeway, Bristol Stadium (Eastville), Twerton Park (1986-96), moved to The Memorial Ground 1996. Record attendance: (Eastville) 38,472, (Twerton Park) 9,813, (Memorial Ground) 12,011
(Total) Current Capacity: 11,916; (4,000 seated*)
Visiting Supporters' Allocation: 1,132 (Centenary Uplands Stand Terrace; open)
Nearest Railway Station: Filton or Stapleton Road
Parking (Car): Limited parking at ground for home fans only; street parking also available
Parking (Coach/Bus): As directed
Police Force and Tel No: Avon/Somerset (0845 456 7000)
Other Clubs Sharing Ground: Bristol Shoguns RUFC
Disabled Visitors' Facilities:
Wheelchairs: 35 wheelchair positions
Blind: Limited provision
Anticipated Development(s): The planned redevelopment of the Memorial Ground with the consequent groundshares for Rovers and Bristol RUFC was deferred during the summer of 2008 as a result of the club's partners in the project pulling out of the scheme to construct a new 18,500-seat ground. If all goes according to plan the club had hoped to start work in the summer of 2009 but the original concept of ground-sharing during the construction phase has been abandoned. In place the ground will now be redeveloped in phases. The first phase, which has yet to start, will see the construction of a 7,000-seat stand at the east end to be followed by a new 2,400-seat South Stand. This work was scheduled for completion by the end of the 2009/10 season after which the remaining two stands will be demolished and replacement North and West stands constructed by the end of the 2010/11 season. Work, however, has yet to start. The entire project is costed at some £35 million.

standing capacity of 8,000 includes 500 on the Family Terrace

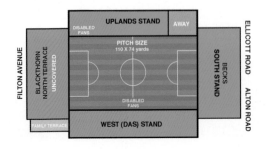

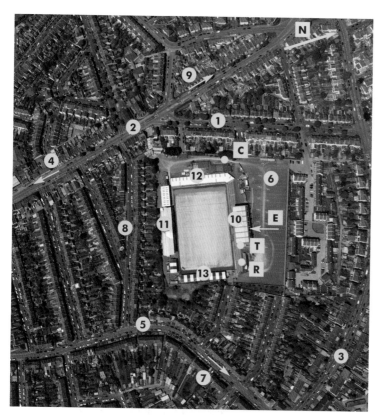

C Rugby Club offices
E Entrance(s) for visiting supporters
R Refrshments for visiting supporters
T Toilets for visiting supporters

1 Filton Avenue
2 Gloucester Road
3 To Muller Road
4 To Bristol city centre (2.5 miles) and Temple Meads station (3 miles)
5 Downer Road
6 Car Park
7 To M32 J2 (1½ miles)
8 Strathmore Road
9 To Filton (1½ miles)
10 Uplands Stand
11 West (Das) Stand
12 Blackthorn North Terrace
13 Becks South Stand

↑ North direction (approx)

◀ 702490
▼ 702508

burnley

Turf Moor, Harry Potts Way, Burnley, Lancashire, BB10 4BX

website: **WWW.BURNLEYFOOTBALLCLUB.COM**
e:mail: **INFO@BURNLEYFC.COM.**
tel no: **0871 221 1882**
colours: **CLARET AND BLUE SHIRTS, WHITE SHORTS**
nickname: **THE CLARETS**
season 2010/11: **CHAMPIONSHIP**

Last Season: **18th** (relegated) (p**38**; w**8**; d**6**; l**24**; gf**42**; ga**82**)

Widely perceived at the start of the season as a cast-iron relegation candidate, initially Burnley's performances, particularly at home – where the team claimed notable scalps in the defeats of Manchester United and Everton – suggested that demotion back to the Championship was perhaps not a foregone conclusion. However, from the end of October, following the 2-0 victory over Hull City, the Clarets won only three of the last 28 League matches. The club's position was not aided by the decision by manager Owen Coyle to take-over at rivals Bolton Wanderers in early January. Burnley moved quickly to appoint ex-Sheffield Wednesday boss Brian Laws to the vacancy – his first managerial appointment at this level. Unfortunately, the club's poor form continued and despite the morale-boosting 4-1 victory at fellow strugglers Hull City – representing three of the only four points won away from Turf Moor all season – the Clarets were relegated following the 4-0 home defeat by Liverpool at the end of April. Defensively, Burnley were poor all season – conceding 82 goals during the campaign (the worst record in the Premier League) — and this frailty will need to be addressed for the 2010/11 season in the Championship. Better placed financially than the other two relegated teams, Burnley ought to have the potential and financial resources to be serious candidates again for the Play-Offs at least.

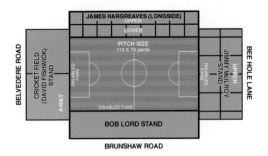

Advanced Tickets No: 0871 221 1914
Fax: 01282 700014
Training Ground: Gawthorpe Hall, off Padiham Road, Padiham, Burnley BB12 8UA
Brief History: Founded 1882, Burnley Rovers (Rugby Club) combined with another Rugby Club, changed to soccer and name to Burnley. Moved from Calder Vale to Turf Moor in 1882. Founder-members Football League (1888). Record attendance 54,775
(Total) Current Capacity: 22,546 all seated)
Visiting Supporters' Allocation: 2,100 in Cricket Field Stand
Nearest Railway Station: Burnley Central
Parking (Car): Church Street and Fulledge Rec. (car parks)
Parking (Coach/Bus): As directed by Police
Police Force and Tel No: Lancashire (0845 125 3545)
Disabled Visitors' Facilities:
Wheelchairs: Places available in North, East and Cricket Field stands
Blind: Headsets provided with commentary
Anticipated Development(s): Planning Permission was granted in late June 2008 for the first phase in the redevelopment of Turf Moor. This will see the construction of a new two-storey building behind the Jimmy McIlroy and Jimmy Hargreaves stands. It had been planned that work on the reconstruction of the Cricket Field (David Fishwick) Stand would commence after the end of the 2008/09 season but work has yet to commence. The new structure will be a single-tier stand accommodating 2,500 costing £10 million. During the stand's construction, away fans will be housed in the lower tier of the Jimmy McIlroy Stand. This work will be followed by the refurbishment of the Bob Lord Stand.

▲ 703146
◀ 703140

C Club Offices
S Club Shop
E Entrance(s) for visiting
supporters

1 Brunshaw Road
2 Belvedere Road
3 Burnley Central station
(½ mile)
4 Cricket Ground
5 Cricket Field Stand
6 East (Jimmy McIlroy) Stand
7 Bob Lord Stand
8 North (James Hargreaves)
Stand

↑ *North direction (approx)*

burton albion

Pirelli Stadium, Princess Way, Burton-on-Trent, Staffordshire DE13 0AR

website: **WWW.BURTONALBIONFC.CO.UK**
e:mail: **BAFC@BURTONALBIONFC.CO.UK**
telephone: **01283 565938**
colours: **YELLOW SHIRTS, BLACK SHORTS**
Nickname: **THE BREWERS**
season 2010/11: **LEAGUE TWO**

Last Season: **13th** (p**46**; w **17**; d **11**; l **18**; gf **71**; ga **71**)

Promoted to the Football League at the end of the 2008/09 season, Burton Albion made a spirited start to their life in League Two and, for a period, it looked as though the team might actually make a sustained challenge for the Play-Offs and as late as early March, with 34 League matches completed, Paul Peschisolido's team was still well-placed in 11th place only six points off the all-important seventh place. However, a run of only three victories in the final 12 League matches will mean that League Two football will again be on offer at the Pirelli Stadium in 2010/11. With the club established in the League, the challenge for the new season will be to maintain progress and push for a good top-half finish at the very least.

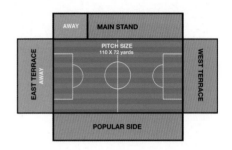

Advance Tickets Tel No: 01283 565938
Fax: 01283 523199
Training Ground: None
Brief History: Burton Albion was founded in 1950 and was promoted to the Football League at the end of the 2008/09 season. Achieving League status means that it is the fourth club from Burton to achieve this feat, following from Burton Swifts (1892-1902), Burton Wanderers (1894-97) and Burton United (1901-07). Previous grounds: Lloyds Foundry and Eton Park (1958-2005). Record attendance (Pirelli Stadium): 6,192
(Total) Current Capacity: 6,912 (2,034 seated)
Visiting Supporters' Allocation: 1,200 on East Terrace plus 300 seated in Main Stand
Nearest Railway Station: Burton-on-Trent (½ mile)
Parking (Car): 400 places at the ground with overflow at adjacent Rykneld Trading Estate
Parking (Coach/Bus): As directed
Police Force and Tel No: Staffordshire (0300 123 4455)
Disabled Visitors' Facilities:
Wheelchairs:
Blind:

C Club offices

1 Princess Way
2 To A38
3 A5121 Derby Road
4 To Burton town centre and
   railway station
5 Car park
6 To A38 and Derby
7 Main Stand
8 Popular Side
9 East Terrace (Away)
10 West Terrace

↑ North direction (approx)

◄ 702609
▾ 702639

bury

Gigg Lane, Gigg Lane, Bury, Lancashire, BL9 9HR

website: **WWW.BURYFC.CO.UK**
e:mail: **INFO@BURYFC.CO.UK**
tel no: **0161 764 4881**
colours: **CLARET/BLUE SHIRTS, WHITE SHORTS**
nickname: **THE SHAKERS**
season 2010/11: **LEAGUE ONE**

Last Season: **9th** (p**46**; w**19**; d**12**; l**15**; gf**54**; ga**59**)

Ultimately a season for huge disappointment for Alan Knill's team, for much of the campaign it looked as though Bury would be a shoo-in for automatic promotion and, if that failed to come off, then a Play-Off place as a consolation prize. As late as mid-February, the Shakers were in a strong second place in the League Two table but results over the last 15 League matches – with the team winning only two of the last 15 League matches and drawing six – meant that even the Play-Offs were missed. However, it was not until the final League Saturday of the season that the team's fate was ultimately determined. One of six teams capable of grabbing the last two Play-Off places, Bury's away draw with Northampton Town was enough to ensure that both teams missed out on the Play-Offs. With Knill promising a major overhaul of the squad for 2010/11, fans will be expecting a much better performance come the new season and the club should again feature in the hunt for the Play-Offs at least.

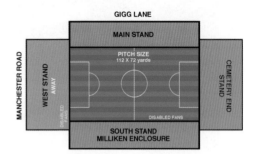

Advance Tickets Tel No: 0161 705 2144
Fax: 0161 764 5521
Training Ground: Lower Gigg, Gigg Lane, Bury BL9 9HR
Brief History: Founded 1885, no former names or former grounds. Record attendance 35,000
(Total) Current Capacity: 11,669 (all seated)
Visiting Supporters' Allocation: 2,000 (all seated) in Manchester Road Stand
Nearest Railway Station: Bury Interchange
Parking (Car): Street parking
Parking (Coach/Bus): As directed by Police
Police Force and Tel No: Greater Manchester (0161 872 5050)
Other clubs sharing ground:
FC United of Manchester
Disabled Visitors' Facilities:
Wheelchairs: South Stand (home) and West Stand (away)
Blind: Commentary available
Anticipated Development(s): The completion of the rebuilt Cemetery End means that current plans for the redevelopment of Gigg Lane have been completed.

C Club Offices
S Club Shop

1 Car Park
2 Gigg Lane
3 A56 Manchester Road
4 To Town Centre & Bury
   Interchange (Metrolink)
   (¾ mile)
5 West (Manchester Road)
   Stand (away)
6 Cemetery End

↑ *North direction (approx)*

◄ 701853
▼ 701863

45

cardiff city

Cardiff City Stadium, Leckwith Road, Cardiff CF11 8AZ

website: **WWW.CARDIFFCITYFC.CO.UK**
e:mail: **CLUB@CARDIFFCITYFC.CO.UK**
tel no: **0845 365 1115**
colours: **BLUE SHIRTS, BLUE SHORTS**
nickname: **THE BLUEBIRDS**
season 2010/11: **CHAMPIONSHIP**

Last Season: **4th** (p**46**; w**22**; d**10**; l**14**; gf**73**; ga**54**)

In the club's first season at its new ground, optimism on the field was tinged with problems off it, as the team's progress up the Championship table was matched by the club's pursuit by HM Revenue and Customs in the High Court. A good start to the season saw the Bluebirds vying for one of the automatic promotion places early on and, although the dream of automatic promotion gradually diminished, the club remained on course for the Play-Offs for virtually the whole season. Finishing in fourth position resulted in a Play-Off semi-final against Leicester City; although David Jones's team won 1-0 away at the Walkers Stadium, a 3-2 home reverse after extra time resulted in the match going to penalties. The home team proved victorious, taking Cardiff back to Wembley for the second time in three seasons. In a pulsating final, Cardiff unfortunately lost to Blackpool 3-2 thus ensuring that Championship football remains on offer in Cardiff in 2010/11. With the end of the season, there is very much a feeling that it marks the end of an era with Peter Ridsdale standing down as chairman and, no doubt, a number of the players moving on to pastures new. With some uncertainty over the club's financial position, failure to achieve the riches offered by the Premier League at the end of the 2009/10 season might prove costly and perhaps the club's best chance for promotion for some years may well have disappeared as well.

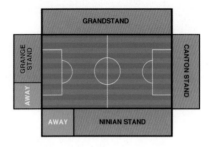

Advance Tickets Tel No: 0845 345 1400

Fax: 0845 365 1116

Training Ground: Vale Hotel, Hensol Park, Hensol CF72 8JY

Brief History: Founded 1899. Former grounds: Riverside Cricket Club, Roath, Sophia Gardens, Cardiff Arms Park and Ninian Park from 1910. Moved to new Cardiff City Stadium in August 2009. Ground record attendance (Ninian Park): 61,566 (Wales v. England, 1961); (at Cardiff City Stadium) 26,033

(Total) Current Capacity: 26,828

Visiting Supporters' Allocation: 1,800 max in corner of Grange and Ninian stands

Nearest Railway Station: Ninian Park (adjacent); Cardiff Central (one mile)

Parking (Car): Adjacent to ground

Parking (Coach/Bus): as directed

Other clubs sharing Ground: Cardiff Blues RUFC

Police Force and Tel No: South Wales (029 2022 2111)

Disabled Visitors' Facilities:

Wheelchairs: 28 spaces in Grandstand

Blind: 80 spaces available

Anticipated Development(s): Following the completion of the new £42 million stadium, the club relocated from its old ground at Ninian Park for the start of the 2009/10 season.

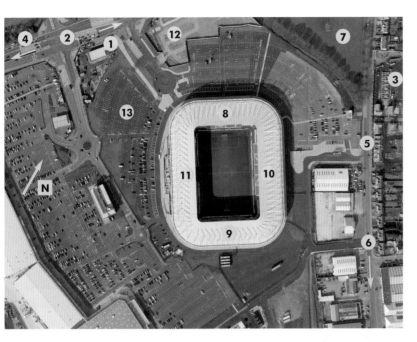

1 To Ninian Park station
  (¼ mile)
2 B4267 Leckwith Road
3 Site of Ninian Park
  (old ground)
4 To A4232 Grangetown Link
5 Sloper Road
6 To city centre and Central
  station
7 Jubilee Park
8 Grange Stand
9 Canton Stand
10 Ninian Stand
11 Grandstand
12 Site for future hotel
13 Car parks

⬆ North direction (approx)

◄ 702793
▼ 702804

carlisle united

Brunton Park, Warwick Road, Carlisle, CA1 1LL

website: **WWW.CARLISLEUNITED.CO.UK**
e:mail: **ENQUIRIES@CARLISLEUNITED.CO.UK**
tel no: **01228 526237**
colours: **BLUE SHIRTS, WHITE SHORTS**
nickname: **THE CUMBRIANS OR THE BLUES**
season 2010/11: **LEAGUE ONE**

Last season **14th** (p**46** w**15** d**13** l**18** gf**63** ga**66**)

In Greg Abbott's first full season in charge at Carlisle United, the team spent the bulk of the campaign in the bottom half of the division, never actually being sucked into the relegation mire but never stringing sufficient results together to result in a sustained push towards the Play-Off zone. Away from the League, however, the team did have some success in becoming the northern finalist for the Johnstone's Paint trophy, defeating Leeds United over the two-leg semi-final on penalties with the scores tied 4-4 on aggregate. This victory took United to Wembley for a final against in-form Southampton and, unfortunately for United fans, the southern team proved too strong, running out 4-1 victors. Another notable cup performance saw the team defeat high-flying Norwich City in the 2nd round of the FA Cup. For 2010/11, United will regard the 14th place achieved at the end of 2009/10 as the springboard for further progress in the new campaign and a strong top-half position should be achievable.

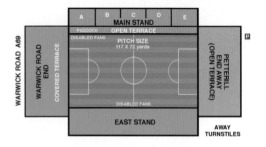

Advance Tickets Tel No: 0844 371 1921
Fax: 01228 554141
Training Ground: Adjacent to main ground
Brief History: Founded 1904 as Carlisle United (previously named Shaddongate United). Former Grounds: Millholme Bank and Devonshire Park, moved to Brunton Park in 1909. Record attendance 27,500

(Total) Current Capacity: 16,981 (6,433 seated)
Visiting Supporters' Allocation: 1,700 (Petterill End Terrace – open – or north end of East Cumberland Building Society Stand)
Nearest Railway Station: Carlisle
Parking (Car): Rear of ground
Parking (Coach/Bus): St Aiden's Road car park
Police Force and Tel No: Cumbria (0345 33 00 247)
Disabled Visitors' Facilities:
Wheelchairs: East Stand and Paddock (prior arrangement)
Blind: No special facilities

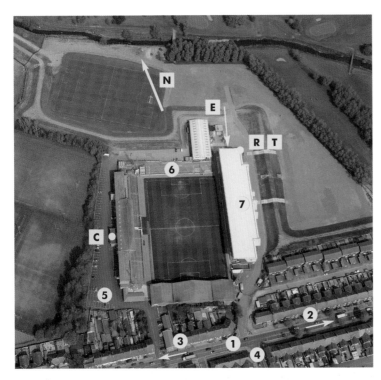

C Club Offices
E Entrance(s) for visiting supporters
R Refreshment bars for visiting supporters
T Toilets for visiting supporters

1 A69 Warwick Road
2 To M6 Junction 43
3 Carlisle Citadel station (1 mile)
4 Greystone Road
5 Car Park
6 Petterill End (away)
7 Cumberland Building Society (East) Stand

⬆ *North direction (approx)*

◀ 701256
▼ 701264

charlton athletic

The Valley, Floyd Road, Charlton, London, SE7 8BL

website: **WWW.CAFC.CO.UK**
e:mail: **CUSTOMERSERVICES@CAFC.CO.UK**
tel no: **020 8333 4000**
colours: **RED SHIRTS, WHITE SHORTS**
nickname: **THE ADDICKS**
season 2010/11: **LEAGUE ONE**

Last Season: **4th** (p**46**; w**23**; d**15**; l**8**; gf**71**; ga**48**)

Relegated at the end of the 2008/09 season, it was widely expected that Phil Parkinson's Charlton Athletic would be amongst the frontrunners for automatic promotion and, with seven wins and two draws in the team's first nine League matches it looked more a case of when rather than if promotion was confirmed. Embarrassingly that period also coincided with a 1-0 away defeat by League Two Hereford United in the 1st round of the Carling Cup. However, from then on the team's League form was variable but the club still retained a mathematical chance of grabbing the second automatic promotion spot – along with Leeds, Millwall, Swindon and Huddersfield – on the last Saturday of the season. Although the Addicks defeated Oldham 2-0, results elsewhere resulted in the team finishing in fourth place and thus facing a Play-Off semi-final against Swindon. Following an aggregate 3-3 draw after extra time, Swindon proved victorious on penalties thus condemning Athletic to a second season in League One. Again, the team ought to be amongst the favourites for automatic promotion but the Play-Offs perhaps represent once more the team's best route back to the Championship.

Advance Tickets Tel No: 0871 226 1905

Fax: 020 8333 4001

Training Ground: Sparrows Lane, New Eltham, London SE9 2JR

Brief History: Founded 1905. Former grounds: Siemens Meadows, Woolwich Common, Pound Park, Angerstein Athletic Ground, The Mount Catford, Selhurst Park (Crystal Palace FC), Boleyn Ground (West Ham United FC), The Valley (1912-23, 1924-85, 1992-date). Founder Members 3rd Division South. Record attendance 75,031

(Total) Current Capacity: 27,111 (all seated)

Visiting Supporters' Allocation: 3,000 (maximum; all seated in South Stand)

Nearest Railway Station: Charlton

Parking (Car): Street parking

Parking (Coach/Bus): As directed by Police

Police Force and Tel No: Metropolitan (0300 123 1212)

Disabled Visitors' Facilities:

Wheelchairs: East/West/South stands

Blind: Commentary, 12 spaces

Anticipated Development(s): The club has Planning Permission for the redevelopment of the East Stand, taking the ground's capacity to 31,000 but there is no confirmed timescale for the work. In December 2006 the club also lodged outline plans for the redevelopment of the rest of the stadium with the intention of taking capacity to 40,600.

E Entrance(s) for visiting
   supporters
R Refreshment bars for visiting
   supporters
T Toilets for visiting supporters

1 Harvey Gardens
2 A206 Woolwich Road
3 Valley Grove
4 Floyd Road
5 Charlton station
6 East Stand
7 North Stand
8 West stand
9 South stand (away)
10 Charlton Church Lane
11 Charlton Lane

↑ North direction (approx)

‹ 701309
▾ 701316

chelsea

Stamford Bridge, Fulham Road, London, SW6 1HS

website: **WWW.CHELSEAFC.COM**
e:mail: **CONTACT VIA WEBSITE**
tel no: **0871 984 1955**
colours: **BLUE SHIRTS, BLUE SHORTS**
nickname: **THE BLUES**
season 2010/11: **PREMIER LEAGUE**

Last Season: **1st** (p**38**; w**27**; d**5**; l**6**; gf**103**; ga**32**)

A hugely successful domestic season for Mario Ancelotti's Chelsea team saw the club win three domestic trophies – the Charity Shield (defeating Manchester United on penalties), the Premier League title (pipping Manchester United to the title) and the FA Cup (with a 1-0 victory over Portsmouth in a match of missed penalties) – but still fail to achieve success in Europe. Having successfully negotiated their way to the Champions League quarter-finals, Chelsea were drawn against Inter Milan under erstwhile manager Jose Mourinho. A 2-1 defeat away in the first leg at the San Siro Stadium seemed to give Chelsea the edge given the away goal. However, the Special One engineered a great performance from his team in the game at Stamford Bridge, winning 1-0 – although Chelsea had had opportunities to score – and a bad night for the home team was compounded by the late sending off of Didier Drogba. Although the League title wasn't confirmed until the final Sunday of the season – a comprehensive 8-0 drubbing of Wigan being a fitting conclusion to the campaign – Chelsea proved themselves prolific scorers, with seven goals in three other League matches. The FA Cup triumph over a weakened Portsmouth was perhaps, however, a swansong for some of the team with a number of players, such as Joe Cole, expected to move in the close season as Ancelotti builds for a new season. Undoubtedly one of the pre-season favourites for domestic success, the club's fulfilment of the Abramovich dream will, however, only be achieved with success on a European stage and the Champions League title.

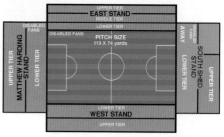

FULHAM ROAD

Advance Tickets Tel No: 0871 984 1905

Fax: 020 7381 4831

Training Ground: 62 Stoke Road, Cobham, Surrey KT11 3PT

Brief History: Founded 1905. Admitted to Football League (2nd Division) on formation. Stamford Bridge venue for F.A. Cup Finals 1919-22. Record attendance 82,905

(Total Current Capacity: 42,449 (all seated)

Visiting Supporters' Allocation: Approx. 1,600 (East Stand Lower; can be increased to 3,200 if required or 5,200 if part of the Matthew Harding Stand [lower tier] is allocated)

Nearest Railway Station: Fulham Broadway or West Brompton

Parking (Car): Street parking and underground car park at ground

Parking (Coach/Bus): As directed by Police

Police Force and Tel No: Metropolitan (0300 123 1212)

Disabled Visitors' Facilities:

Wheelchairs: East Stand

Blind: No special facility

Anticipated Development(s): Faced by the competing clubs building ever larger grounds, Chelsea is conscious that the existing 42,000-seat capacity at Stamford Bridge is too small but difficult to increase. As a result the club is examining the possibility of relocation, with a number of sites (including the erstwhile Lillie Bridge cricket ground now used as the Seagrave Road car park as one option). There is, however, no definite plan as yet nor any timetable for the work if it were to proceed.

1 A304 Fulham Road
2 To Central London
3 Fulham Broadway
  tube station
4 Matthew Harding Stand
5 East Stand
6 West Stand
7 South (Shed) Stand
8 West Brompton Station

↑ North direction (approx)

◄ 701425
▼ 701421

cheltenham town

Abbey Business Stadium, Whaddon Road, Cheltenham, Gloucestershire GL52 5NA

website: **WWW.CTFC.COM**
e:mail: **INFO@CTFC.COM**
tel no: **01242 573558**
colours: **RED SHIRTS, RED SHORTS**
nickname: **THE ROBINS**
season 2010/11: **LEAGUE TWO**

Last Season: **22nd** (p**46**; w**10**; d**18**; l**18**; gf**54**; ga**71**)

Following an allegation of racially abusing a nightclub bouncer in October 2009, Martin Allen was placed on gardening leave by the Robins; although the allegations were later proved to be unfounded and no further action was taken by the local police, the manager was to depart from Whaddon Road in mid-December by mutual consent. During Allen's absence, John Schofield acted as caretaker manager until the appointment of ex-Kidderminster boss, Mark Yates, as the new permanent manager just before Christmas. Under Yates, the club's form was patchy and the team remained hovering just outside the bottom two for all of the second half of the season. Mathematically, the club's League Two survival was not guaranteed until the final Saturday of the season, although the team's better goal difference than Grimsby Town meant that the Lincolnshire team looked doomed. In the event a 1-1 home draw against Accrington Stanley in the final League match of the season was more than enough to secure safety given Grimsby's defeat but, unless the squad is significantly strengthened in the close season, it looks as though the Robins will face a hard battle to retain League status come May 2011.

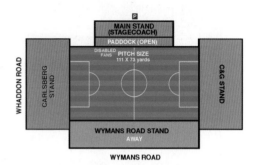

Advance Tickets Tel No: 01242 573558

Fax: 01242 224675

Training Ground: Cheltenham Town FC Training Complex, Quat Goose Lane, Swindon Village, Cheltenham GL51 9RX

Brief History: Cheltenham Town was founded in 1892. The club moved to Whaddon Road in 1932, having previously played at Carter's Field. After two seasons in the Conference the club achieved Nationwide League status at the end of the 1998/99 season. Record attendance 8,326

(Total Current Capacity: 7,066 (3,912 seated)

Visiting Supporters' Allocation: 1,100 all-seated in Wymans Road Stand

Nearest Railway Station: Cheltenham (1.5 miles)

Parking (Car): Limited parking at ground; otherwise on-street

Parking (Coach/Bus): As directed by Police

Police Force and Tel No: Gloucestershire (0845 090 1234)

Disabled Visitors' Facilities:
Wheelchairs: 68 wheelchair spaces
Blind: No special facility

Anticipated Development(s): The Carlsberg Stand – which replaced the open Whaddon Road Terrace – was opened in December 2005. This structure provides seats for 1,000 fans. The next phase in the development of Whaddon Road will involve the rebuilding of the Main Stand, but there is at present no timescale for this work.

C Club Offices
E Entrance(s) for visiting
  supporters

1 B4632 Prestbury Road
2 Cromwell Road
3 Whaddon Road
4 Wymans Road
5 To B4075 Priors Road
6 To B4075 Priors Road
7 To Cheltenham town centre
  and railway station (1.5 and
  2 miles respectively)
8 Main Stand
9 Wymans Road Stand
10 Prestbury Road End
11 Carlsberg Stand (away)

↑ *North direction (approx)*

◄ 702510
▼ 702529

chesterfield

b2net Stadium, 1866 Sheffield Road, Chesterfield S41 8NZ

website: **WWW.CHESTERFIELD–FC.CO.UK**
e:mail: **SUEGREEN@CHESTERFIELD–FC.CO.UK**
tel no: **01246 209765***
colours: **BLUE AND WHITE SHIRTS, WHITE SHORTS**
nickname: **THE SPIREITES**
season 2010/11: **LEAGUE TWO**

Last Season: **8th** (p**46**; w**21**; d**7**; l**18**; gf**61**; ga**62**)

In the club's last season at its historic Saltergate ground, the team's home for almost 130 years, hopes were high that John Sheridan's Chesterfield would improve on the 10th place achieved at the end of the 2008/09 season and make a much more sustained push towards promotion and the Play-Offs. With the season three-quarters completed towards the end of February, the Spireites looked to be sitting pretty in fourth place, one point out of the automatic promotion places and 11 points clear of Dagenham in eighth. However, a dismal run in the final 14 League games saw the team win only three and draw four of the last 14 matches, although the club retained a mathematical chance of nicking one of the last two Play-Off places even on the final Saturday of the season. However, a 2-1 victory over promoted Bournemouth in the last match ever to be played at Saltergate was not sufficient and so the new b2net Stadium will make its debut in League Two. Chesterfield, with the confidence engendered by its new home, ought once again to be amongst the favourites to reach the Play-Offs at least in 2010/11.

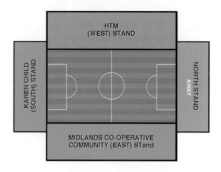

Advance Tickets Tel No: 01246 209765*
Fax: 01246 556799*
Training Ground: No special facility
Brief History: Founded 1867. Former grounds: Spital Vale and Saltergate; moved to new b2net Stadium for start of the 2010/11 season. Formerly named Chesterfield Town. Record attendance (at Saltergate) 30,968
(Total) Current Capacity: 10,338
Visiting Supporters' Allocation: TBC on North Stand
Nearest Railway Station: Chesterfield
Parking (Car): As directed
Parking (Coach/Bus): As directed
Police Force and Tel No: Derbyshire Constabulary (0345 123 33 33)
Disabled Visitors' Facilities:
Wheelchairs: tbc
Blind: tbc
Anticipated Development(s): Work started on the construction of the new b2net Stadium, on the site of the erstwhile Deva Glass Works, in the summer of 2009. It is planned that the new 10,338-seat stadium will be completed for the start of the 2010/11 season.

* Telephone numbers for Saltergate and may change with relocation (although the club has indicated that it intends to retain the existing numbers)

1 A61
2 To Sheffield
3 A61 to town centre and railway station (one mile)
4 A619 Rother Way
5 Lockoford Road
6 B5057 Sheffield Road
7 Peveril Road
8 North Stand
9 West Stand
10 South Stand
11 East Stand
12 Supermarket`

⬆ North direction (approx)

◀ 702926
▼ 702937

colchester united

Weston Homes Community Stadium, United Way, Colchester CO4 5UP

website: **WWW.CU–FC.COM**
e:mail: **CAROLINE@COLCHESTERUNITED.NET**
tel no: **01206 755100**
colours: **BLUE AND WHITE SHIRTS, WHITE SHORTS**
nickname: **THE U'S**
season 2010/11: **LEAGUE ONE**

Last Season: **8th** (p**46**; w**20**; d**12**; l**14**; gf**64**; ga**52**)

A sublime start to the season saw United inflict a 7-1 defeat on newly-relegated Norwich City at Carrow Road; it was, however, a result that was to have unforeseen consequences in Essex as, following Bryan Gunn's dismissal later in the week, Norwich came calling for U's boss Paul Lambert as Gunn's replacement. Jo Dunne was appointed caretaker manager before Aidy Boothroyd – the ex-Watford boss – was appointed to the position. Under Boothroyd the club initially prospered, being one of the teams in the hunt for automatic promotion at the end of February when the team stood in third place, one point behind Leeds United and 10 above Millwall in seventh. However, an appalling late run of form – two wins and four draws in the club's final 14 League matches – saw the team drop to a disappointing eighth, eight points off Huddersfield in sixth place, come the end of the season. With the campaign over, Boothroyd departed to take over as new boss at Coventry City and new manager John Ward will face the challenge of re-establishing United as a force in League One. Potentially again a Play-Off candidate in 2010/11 but much will depend on the new manager and who he is able to bring in.

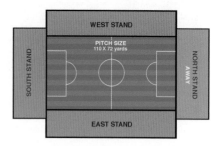

Advance Tickets Tel No: 0845 437 9089
Fax: 01206 755 114
Training Ground: No special facility (moving to new facility during season)
Brief History: Founded 1937, joined Football League 1950, relegated 1990 to Conference, promoted back to the Football League 1992. Played at Layer Road until end of 2007/08 season. Record attendance (at Layer Road) 19,072; (at Weston Homes Community Stadium) 9,559
(Total) Current Capacity: 10,083 (all seated)
Visiting Supporters' Allocation: 1,900 (North Stand)
Nearest Railway Station: Colchester main line (two miles)
Parking (Car): 600 spaces at ground
Parking (Coach/Bus): As directed
Police Force and Tel No: Essex (0800 333 4444)
Disabled Visitors' Facilities:
Wheelchairs: 100 wheelchair places
Blind: No special facility
Anticipated Development(s): Following a number of years planning for relocation, the club played its final season at its old Layer Road ground in 2007/08 and relocated to the new £14 million 10,000-seat stadium for the start of the 2008/09 campaign. The ground is designed to allow for expansion to 18,000 if the need arises.

1 A12
2 Towards intersection with
   new northern link road
   and Ipswich
3 Towards London
4 To Colchester town centre
   (three miles) and Colchester
   main line station
5 North Stand (away)
6 East Stand
7 West Stand
8 South Stand

↑ *North direction (approx)*

◄ 701440
▼ 701468

coventry city

The Ricoh Arena, Phoenix Way, Foleshill, Coventry CV6 6GE

website: **WWW.CCFC.CO.UK**
e:mail: **CUSTOMER.SERVICES@CCFC.CO.UK**
tel no: **0844 873 1883**
colours: **SKY BLUE SHIRTS, SKY BLUE SHORTS**
nickname: **THE SKY BLUES**
season 2010/11: **CHAMPIONSHIP**

Last Season: **19th** (p**46**; w**13**; d**15**; l**18**; gf**47**; ga**64**)

Another difficult season at the Reebok Stadium saw Coventry City finish in a disappointing 19th position and resulted in Chris Coleman's dismissal as City's boss after two-and-a-half years in charge following the final match of the season – a 4-0 home defeat by fellow strugglers Watford. Although the season started with some promise – despite the 1-0 home defeat by Hartlepool in the 1st round of the Carling Cup – with the team in 10th place at the end of September, a run of 11 matches without a win sent the team tumbling down the table and the problem was further compounded by a disastrous run at the end of the campaign when the team went a further 11 League matches without a win, gaining only five points during the period. The new manager – the experienced Aidy Boothroyd from Colchester United – will face the challenge of trying to keep City in the Championship; it's now almost a decade since City last graced the Premier League and, although the ground is undoubtedly of top-flight quality, the football on its pitch hasn't been in recent seasons. In City's nine seasons thus far at this level, the club has struggled to get above a position of mid-table and a further battle to keep Championship-level football looks likely in 2010/11.

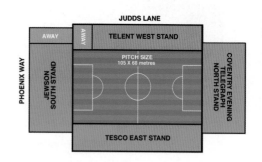

Advance Tickets Tel No: 0844 873 1883
Fax: 0844 873 6301
Training Ground: Sky Blue Lodge, Leamington Road, Ryton-on-Dunsmore, Coventry CV8 3EL
Brief History: Founded 1883 as Singers FC, changed name to Coventry City in 1898. Former grounds: Dowell's Field, Stoke Road Ground and Highfield Road (1899-2005) moved to new ground for start of the 2005/06 season. Record attendance (at Highfield Road): 51,455; (at Ricoh Arena): 31,407
(Total) Current Capacity: 32,500 (All seated)
Visiting Supporters' Allocation: 3,000 in corner of Jewson South and Telent West Stands
Nearest Railway Station: Coventry (three miles)
Parking (Car): As directed
Parking (Coach/Bus): As directed
Police Force and Tel No: West Midlands (0345 113 5000)
Disabled Visitors' Facilities:
Wheelchairs: 102 spaces (including 27 away) at pitchside or raised platform
Blind: No special facility at present but under negotiation
Anticipated Development(s): With the completion of the Ricoh Stadium there are no further plans for development at the present time. There is still no news about the construction of a possible station on the Coventry-Nuneaton railway line.

▲ 702554
◄ 702564

1 Judds Lane
2 Rowley's Green Lane
3 A444 Phoenix Way
4 To Coventry city centre
   and railway station
   (three miles)
5 Coventry-Nuneaton
   railway line
6 To M6 Junction 3 (one mile)
   and Nuneaton
7 Telent West Stand
8 Coventry Evening Telegraph
   North Stand
9 Tesco East Stand
10 Jewson South Stand
11 Exhibition hall

↑ North direction (approx)

crewe alexandra

The Alexandra Stadium, Gresty Road, Crewe, Cheshire, CW2 6EB

website: **WWW.CREWEALEX.NET**
e:mail: **INFO@CREWEALEX.NET**
tel no: **01270 213014**
colours: **RED SHIRTS, WHITE SHORTS**
nickname: **THE RAILWAYMEN**
season 2010/11: **LEAGUE TWO**

Last Season: **18th** (p**46**; w**15**; d**10**; l**21**; gf**68**; ga**73**)

Following relegation at the end of the 2008/09 season, hopes were high at Gresty Road that Crewe would make a serious attempt at an immediate return to League One. However, a disappointing start to the campaign, which saw the team stand in 15th place after a 3-2 home defeat by Bury saw manager Gudjon Thordarson sacked in early October after only nine months in the job. He was replaced as caretaker boss by long-time manager Dario Gradi. Thereafter the club's League form was variable with the club never managing to climb above a position of mid-table mediocrity. Moreover the end of the season, with three victories out of the last 15 matches does not bode well. It wasn't just in the League that Crewe struggled as a 3-2 defeat away at non-League York City in the 1st round of the FA Cup indicated. For the new season fans will be expecting a much more sustained push towards promotion. Over the years, Crewe and Dario Gradi have put together some impressive teams playing attractive football; there will be hopes at Gresty Road that this tradition can be restored.

Advance Tickets Tel No: 01270 252610

Fax: 01270 216320

Training Ground: Details omitted at club's request

Brief History: Founded 1877. Former Grounds: Alexandra Recreation Ground (Nantwich Road), Earle Street Cricket Ground, Edleston Road, Old Sheds Fields, Gresty Road (Adjacent to current Ground), moved to current Ground in 1906. Founder members of 2nd Division (1892) until 1896. Founder members of 3rd Division North (1921). Record attendance 20,000

(Total) Current Capacity: 10,066 (all seated)

Visiting Supporters' Allocation: 1,680
(Blue Bell BMW Stand)

Nearest Railway Station: Crewe

Parking (car): There is a car park adjacent to the ground. It should be noted that there is a residents' only scheme in operation in the streets surrounding the ground.

Parking (Coach/Bus): As directed by Police

Police Force and Tel No: Cheshire (0845 458 0000)

Disabled Visitors' Facilities:

Wheelchairs: Available on all four sides

Blind: Commentary available

Anticipated Development(s): The club has long term plans for the construction of a new two-tier stand to replace the Blue Bell (BMW) Stand, although there is no confirmed timescale for the work.

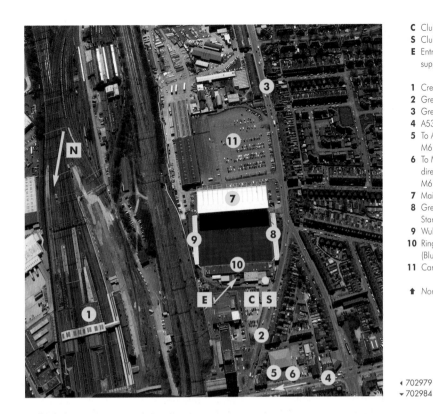

C Club Offices
S Club Shop
E Entrance(s) for visiting
  supporters

1 Crewe BR Station
2 Gresty Road
3 Gresty Road
4 A534 Nantwich Road
5 To A5020 to
  M6 Junction 16
6 To M6 Junction 17 [follow
  directions at roundabout to
  M6 J16/J17]
7 Main (Air Products) Stand
8 Gresty Road (AB Nutrition)
  Stand
9 Wulvern Housing Stand
10 Ringways Stand
  (Blue Bell BMW) (away)
11 Car Park

⬆ North direction (approx)

◄ 702979
▼ 702984

crystal palace

Selhurst Park Stadium, Whitehorse Lane, London, SE25 6PU

website: **WWW.CPFC.CO.UK**
e:mail: **INFO@CPFC.CO.UK**
tel no: **020 8768 6000**
colours: **BLUE AND RED STRIPED SHIRTS, BLUE SHORTS**
nickname: **THE EAGLES (historically the Glaziers)**
season 2010/11: **CHAMPIONSHIP**

Last Season: **21st*** (p**46**; w**14**; d**17**; l**15**; gf**50**; ga**53**)

Struggling financially for a number of years and with a transfer ban already in force, Crystal Palace became the first club to go into Administration during the 2009/10 season when, in late January, the Eagles finally succumbed. With the automatic 10-point deduction, the team went from Play-Off chasers to battlers against relegation. In early March, following a period of speculation, Neil Warnock departed as manager to take over as boss at rivals QPR; the club's administrators moved quickly to appoint Paul Hart, who'd already managed Portsmouth and QPR during the season, to the vacancy until the end of the season. Ultimately the club's fate rested on the final Sunday of the season with the away trip to Sheffield Wednesday; win or draw and Palace were safe at their host's expense but defeat meant relegation. Securing a 2-1 lead approaching full-time suggested that Hart's team would survive but, with minutes left, Wednesday equalised. With all the pressure now coming from the home team, the five minutes of added time must have felt like an eternity to the away fans. However, although Wednesday came close to snatching a victory, Palace held on and so, despite the handicap of the 10-point deduction, can plan for another season in the Championship. With the club's future assured, although it was a close run affair, and a new manager — George Burley — appointed, fans of the club can now perhaps look forward to the new season with more optimism. Consolidation in the Championship must, however, be the first priority.

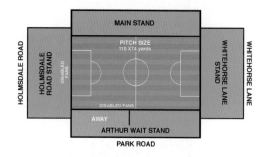

Advance Tickets Tel No: 08712 000071
Fax: 020 8771 5311
Ticket Office/Fax: 020 8653 4708
Training Ground: Copers Cope Road, Beckenham BR3 1RJ
Brief History: Founded 1905. Former Grounds: The Crystal Palace (F.A. Cup Finals venue), London County Athletic Ground (Herne Hill), The Nest (Croydon Common Athletic Ground), moved to Selhurst Park in 1924. Founder members 3rd Division (1920). Record attendance 51,482
(Total) Current Capacity: 26,309 (all seated)
Visiting Supporters' Allocation: Approx 2,000 in Arthur Wait Stand
Nearest Railway Station: Selhurst, Norwood Junction and Thornton Heath
Parking (Car): Street parking and Sainsbury's car park
Parking (Coach/Bus): Thornton Heath
Police Force and Tel No: Metropolitan (0300 123 1212)
Disabled Visitors' Facilities:
Wheelchairs: 56 spaces in Arthur Wait and Holmesdale Stands
Blind: Commentary available
Anticipated Development(s): Although the club had plans to reconstruct the Main Stand — indeed had Planning Permission for the work — local opposition has meant that no work has been undertaken. Both the ground and the club are now owned by the same company created to take the club out of Administration.

* 10 points deducted for going into Administration during the course of the season

C Club Offices
S Club Shop
E Entrance(s) for visiting supporters
T Toilets for visiting supporters

1 Whitehorse Lane
2 Park Road
3 Arthur Wait Stand
4 Norwood Junction station (¼ mile)
5 Selhurst station (½ mile)
6 Thornton Heath station (½ mile)
7 Car Park (Sainsbury's)

⬆ *North direction (approx)*

◀ 701550
▼ 701566

dagenham and redbridge

London Borough of Barking & Dagenham Stadium, Victoria Road, Dagenham, Essex, RM10 7XL

website: **WWW.DAGGERS.CO.UK**
e:mail: **INFO@DAGGERS.CO.UK**
tel no: **020 8592 1549**
colours: **RED AND BLUE SHIRTS, BLUE SHORTS**
nickname: **THE DAGGERS**
season 2010/11: **LEAGUE ONE**

Last Season: **7th** (promoted) (p**46**; w**20**; d**12**; l**14**; gf**69**; ga**58**)

A good start to the season saw John Still's Dagenham & Redbridge team amongst the early pacemakers and, with half the season gone, the club was safely ensconced in one of the automatic promotion places. However, a run of only three victories in 12 matches from the end of January saw the club drift into mid-table by the middle of March. Five wins and a draw in the club's final seven League matches were sufficient, however, to bring a Play-Off place although this wasn't confirmed until the final Saturday when the Daggers were one of six clubs retaining a mathematical chance of grabbing the two remaining Play-Off spots. A 2-0 victory away at already relegated Darlington made results elsewhere immaterial and brought a Play-Off semi-final against Morecambe. Winning 6-0 in the first leg gave the Daggers an undoubted edge and, despite Morecambe's 2-1 win in the return match, Dagenham set up a final against Rotherham at Wembley. In a dramatic match, Still's team emerged victorious 3-2 to bring League One football to Victoria Road for the first time. Realistically, however, with average attendance of just over 2,000, the Daggers are at an immense disadvantage in a division that includes teams of the size of Charlton, Huddersfield and Sheffield Wednesday. Undoubtedly one of the pre-season favourites for relegation, anything from 20th and above could be considered a triumph.

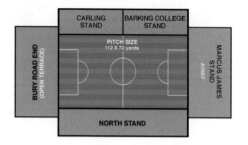

Advance Tickets Tel No: 020 8592 1549
Fax: 020 8593 7227
Training Ground: Details omitted at Club's request
Brief History: The club has roots in four earlier clubs: Ilford (1881); Leytonstone (1886); Walthamstow Avenue (1900); and Dagenham (1949). Ilford and Leytonstone merged in 1979 and, in 1988, became Redbridge Forest following the incorporation of Walthamstow Avenue. Redbridge Forest moved to Victoria Road in 1991 and formed Dagenham & Redbridge with Dagenham in 1992. Promoted to the Football League at the end of the 2006/07 season. Record attendance (at the Victoria Ground): 7,200; (as Dagenham & Redbridge): 5,949
(Total) Current Capacity: 6,078 (2,200 seats)
Visiting Supporters' Allocation: 1,200 (all seated) in Marcus James Stand
Nearest Railway Station: Dagenham East (District Line)
Parking (Car): car park at ground or on-street
Parking (Coach/Bus): As directed
Police Force and Tel No: Metropolitan (0300 123 1212)
Disabled Visitors' Facilities:
Wheelchairs: 10 spaces at Pondfield End of Main Stand
Blind: No specific facility
Anticipated Development(s): Work on the construction of the new 1,200-seat covered stand at the Pondfield Road End was completed early in the 2009/10 season and first used for the match against Bradford City at the end of October. The new accommodation forms the away end at the ground.

1 A1112 North Rainham Road
2 Dagenham East
  Underground station
3 Oxlow Lane
4 Victoria Road
5 Bury Road
6 Surrey Road
7 North Stand
8 Bury Road Stand
9 Carling Stand
10 Marcus James Stand (away)
11 Family Stand

↑ *North direction (approx)*

◄ 703158
▼ 703161

derby county

Pride Park, Derby, Derbyshire, DE24 8XL

website: **WWW.DCFC.CO.UK**
e:mail: **DERBY.COUNTY@DCFC.CO.UK**
tel no: **0871 472 1884**
colours: **WHITE SHIRTS, BLACK SHORTS**
nickname: **THE RAMS**
season 2010/11: **CHAMPIONSHIP**

Last Season: **14th** (p**46**; w**15**; d**11**; l**20**; gf**53**; ga**63**)

A difficult first full season for Nigel Clough at Derby saw the club struggle to make an impact in the Championship; a rocky start to the season resulted in the team more interested about events at the bottom of the table rather than the top. And it wasn't only in the League that the Rams struggled, as the 2-1 defeat away at League Two Rotherham United in the 1st round of the Carling cup emphasised. Form later in the season, with three wins and five draws in the last 10 League matches, might indicate that Clough and the team have turned the corner although fans will still need convincing next season that Clough is the right man to see County threaten to take the step towards the Play-Offs. Much will depend on the squad that Clough is able to retain and build on in the close season. Derby ought to have the potential to reach the Play-Offs at least but a top-half finish is perhaps a more realistic expectation.

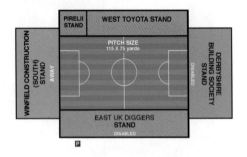

Advance Tickets Tel No: 0871 472 1884
Fax: 01332 667540
Training Ground: Moor Farm Training Centre, Morley Road, Oakwood, Derby DE21 4TB
Brief History: Founded 1884. Former grounds: The Racecourse Ground, the Baseball Ground (1894-1997), moved to Pride Park 1997. Founder members of the Football League (1888). Record attendance at the Baseball Ground: 41,826; at Pride Park: 33,297
(Total) Current Capacity: 33,597
Visiting Supporters' Allocation: 5,600 maximum in the South (Winfield Construction) Stand
Nearest Railway Station: Derby
Parking (Car): 2,300 places at the ground designated for season ticket holders. Also two 1,000 car parks on the A6/A52 link road. No on-street parking
Parking (Coach/Bus): As directed
Police Force and Tel No: Derbyshire (0345 123 3333)
Disabled Visitors' Facilities:
Wheelchairs: 70 home/30 away spaces
Blind: Commentary available
Anticipated Development(s): Although formal proposals have yet to be lodged with the planning authorities, the club is planning a £20 million scheme for a hotel, shops and offices adjacent to Pride Park. There are also plans for the expansion of the ground's capacity to 44,000 via the construction of second tiers on the East, North and South stands. There is however, no time-scale for the work.

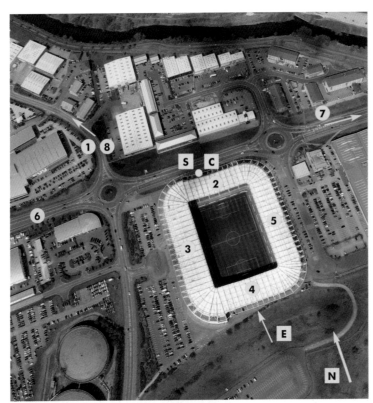

C Club Offices
S Club Shop
E Entrance(s) for visiting
   supporters

1 To Derby Midland station
2 North Stand
3 Toyota West Stand
4 South (Winfield Construction)
   Stand (away)
5 UK Diggers East Stand
6 Derwent Parade
7 To A52/M1
8 To City Centre and A6

↑ North direction (approx)

◄ 702991
▼ 703002

doncaster rovers

Keepmoat Stadium, Stadium Way, Lakeside, Doncaster DN4 5JW

website: **WWW.DONCASTERROVERSFC.CO.UK**
e:mail: **INFO@DONCASTERROVERSFC.CO.UK**
tel no: **01302 764664**
colours: **RED AND WHITE SHIRTS, BLACK SHORTS**
nickname: **THE ROVERS**
season 2010/11: **CHAMPIONSHIP**

Last Season: **12th** (p**46**; w**15**; d**15**; l**16**; gf**59**; ga**58**)

In the club's second season in the Championship, Sean O'Driscoll's side started the campaign poorly with only one win in the first 12 League matches and a position just above the drop zone. However, the club's form improved immeasurably from late October onwards and towards the end of the season the team was within striking distance of claiming an unexpected place in the Play-Offs. One factor in the club's advance up the Championship table was the scoring prowess of on-loan striker Billy Sharp from Sheffield United. The challenge for 2010/11 will be to build upon the foundations laid in 2009/10. The reality, however, is that Rovers are punching above their weight at this level despite the retention of Sharp, acquired for a club record fee. The reality is that Rovers may well struggle to retain Championship status come May 2011.

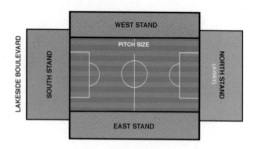

Advance Tickets Tel No: 01302 762576
Fax: 01302 363525
Training Ground: Cantley Park, Aintree Avenue, Doncaster DN4 6HR
Brief History: Founded 1879. Former grounds: Town Moor, Belle Vue (not later ground), Deaf School Playing Field (later name Intake Ground), Bennetthorpe, Belle Vue (1922-2006). Returned to Football League after a five-year absence in 2003. Record attendance (at Belle Vue) 37,149; (at Keepmoat Stadium) 15,001
(Total) Current Capacity: 15,231
Visiting Supporters' Allocation: 3,350 (North Stand)
Nearest Railway Station: Doncaster (two miles)
Parking (Car): 1,000 place car park at ground
Parking (Coach/Bus): As directed
Other Clubs Sharing Ground: Doncaster Dragons RLFC and Doncaster Belles Ladies FC
Police Force and Tel No: South Yorkshire (0114 220 2020)
Disabled Visitors' Facilities:
Wheelchairs: Three sides of ground (16-18 at pitch side)
Blind: Commentary available
Anticipated Development(s): The club moved into the new Keepmoat Stadium during the course of the 2006/07 season. The ground, which cost £21 million to construct, is owned by Doncaster Council. There are no plans for further development at this stage.

1 Lakeside Boulevard
2 To A6182 White Rose Way
3 To Doncaster town centre
  and railway station
4 To Junction 3 M18
5 Athletics Stadium
6 Car park
7 North Stand (away)
8 West Stand
9 East Stand
10 South Stand

↑ North direction (approx)

‹ 703003
▾ 703006

everton

Goodison Park, Liverpool L4 4EL

website: **WWW.EVERTONFC.COM**
e:mail: **EVERTON@EVERTONFC.COM**
tel no: **0871 663 1878**
colours: **BLUE AND WHITE SHIRTS, WHITE SHORTS**
nickname: **THE TOFFEES**
season 2010/11: **PREMIER LEAGUE**

Last Season: **8th (p38; w16; d13; l9; gf60; ga49)**

Having finished fifth at the end of the 2008/09 season, David Moyes' Everton team faced competition both at home and, courtesy of the Europa League, in Europe. With the loss of key players to injury for large parts of the season, battling on two fronts was always, perhaps, going to be a struggle for the team and, although reaching the round of 32 in the Europa League (where the Toffees went out 4-2 on aggregate to Sporting Lisbon), the form domestically was never sufficient to suggest that the team was capable of threatening a repeat of the sustained push towards a top-four position. A late run of six wins and five draws in the club's final 11 League matches suggests, however, that with key players restored to the squad, Everton are a team capable of improvement in 2010/11 provided that Moyes doesn't lose key members of his squad – and there are rumours that several members of the team may move during the close season – and is able to recruit judiciously. Everton ought to have the potential for finish in the top six or seven and, without the distraction of European competition in 2010/11, ought perhaps to make a better attempt at the domestic cup competitions.

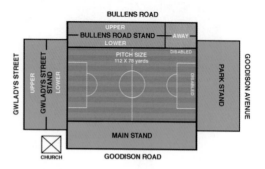

Advance Tickets Tel No: 0871 663 1878
Fax: 0151 286 9112
Training Ground: Bellefield Training Ground, Sandforth Road, West Derby, Liverpool L12 1LW
Tel: 0151 330 2278
Fax: 0151 284 5181
Brief History: Founded 1879 as St. Domingo, changed to Everton in 1880. Former grounds: Stanley Park, Priory Road and Anfield (Liverpool F.C. ground), moved to Goodison Park in 1892. Founder-members Football League (1888). Record attendance 78,299
(Total) Current Capacity: 40,569 (all seated)
Visiting Supporters' Allocation: 3,000 (part of Bullens Road Stand) maximum
Nearest Railway Station: Kirkdale
Parking (Car): Corner of Utting Avenue and Priory Road
Parking (Coach/Bus): Priory Road
Police Force and Tel No: Merseyside (0151 709 6010)
Disabled Visitors' Facilities:
Wheelchairs: Bullens Road Stand
Blind: Commentary available
Anticipated Development(s): The club's plans for relocating to a new £400 million stadium at Kirkby were rejected in November 2009. Following this, the club decided to review its options either to relocate or to redevelop Goodison Park and has held discussions with the local authorities in order to progress matters.

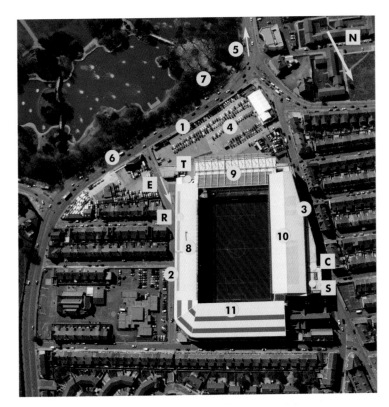

C Club Offices
S Club Shop
E Entrance(s) for visiting
  supporters
R Refreshment bars for visiting
  supporters
T Toilets for visiting supporters

1 A580 Walton Road
2 Bullens Road
3 Goodison Road
4 Car Park
5 Liverpool Lime Street station
  (2 miles)
6 To M57 Junction 2,
  4 and 5
7 Stanley Park
8 Bullens Road Stand
9 Park Stand
10 Main Stand
11 Gwladys Stand

⬆ North direction (approx)

◄ 702072
▼ 702042

exeter city

St James Park, Stadium Way, Exeter, EX4 6PX

website: **WWW.EXETERCITYFC.CO.UK**
e:mail: **RECEPTION@EXETERCITYFC.CO.UK**
tel no: **01392 411243**
colours: **RED AND WHITE SHIRTS, WHITE SHORTS**
nickname: **THE GRECIANS**
season 2010/11: **LEAGUE ONE**

For much of the campaign it looked as though two promotions in two successive seasons might prove too much for Paul Tisdale's Exeter City outfit as the Grecians struggled against the drop for much of the season. In mid-March with 11 games left and with the club in 21st place four points adrift from safety, it looked as though the doom merchants were going to be proved correct but a late run of form with a run of only one defeat in the last 12 matches leading up to the home fixture against Huddersfield Town meant that everything came down to results on the final day with five clubs – Orient, Tranmere Rovers, Hartlepool United and City – all mathematically capable of facing the drop. Of the five, City had perhaps the trickiest task, facing an inform Huddersfield Team with the latter still with a mathematical – if improbable – chance of automatic promotion. As it was, fate brought the battle down ultimately to Gillingham – who were losing to Wycombe – and City with the latter favourites for the drop as the match remained tied at 1-1 until the 82nd minute when Ryan Harley scored a late winner for the Grecians to condemn Gillingham to League Two. For 2010/11 Exeter may well again struggle to retain League One but having battled once and survived, the team will be better equipped to make a success of it.

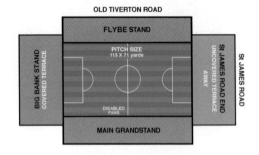

Advance Tickets Tel No: 01392 411423
Fax: 01392 413959
Training Ground: Cat & Fiddle Training Ground, Sidmouth Road, Clyst St Mary, Exeter EX5 1DP
Brief History: Founded in 1904 as a result of the amalgamation of St Sidwell United and Exeter United. Founder members of Third Division (1920). Relegated to Conference 2003; League status reclaimed 2008. Record attendance 20,984
(Total) Current Capacity: 9,036 (3,806 seated)
Visiting Supporters' Allocation: 1,200 (St James' Road End – open terrace) plus limited seats in Grandstand.
Nearest Railway Station: Exeter St James Park
Parking (Car): National Car Park or council car parks (no on-street parking; residents' only scheme in operation)
Parking (Coach/Bus): Paris Street bus station
Police Force and Tel No: Devon & Cornwall (08452 777444)
Disabled Visitors' Facilities:
Wheelchairs: 40 places in Flybe Stand and Big Bank
Blind: No special facility
Anticipated Development(s):

E Entrance(s) for visiting
 supporters

1 Exeter St James Park station
2 St James Road
3 Old Tiverton Road
4 Big Bank Stand
5 Flybe Stand
6 St James Terrace (away)
7 Grandstand

↑ North direction (approx)

◄ 702817
▼ 702824

fulham

Craven Cottage, Stevenage Road, Fulham, London SW6 6HH

website: **WWW.FULHAMFC.COM**
e:mail: **ENQUIRIES@FULHAMFC.COM**
tel no: **0870 442 1222**
colours: **WHITE SHIRTS, BLACK SHORTS**
nickname: **THE COTTAGERS**
season 2010/11: **PREMIER LEAGUE**

Last Season: **12th** (p**38**; w**12**; d**10**; l**16**; gf**39**; ga**46**)

Although not quite hitting the heights of 2008/09, Fulham can still look back on the 2009/10 season with some satisfaction. Under Roy Hodgson, the club's position in the Premier League looked secure. For the Craven Cottage faithful, however, the real story of the past season was the club's unprecedented success in reaching the final of the Europa League. Amongst the team's victims during the course of a long cup run were the competition's winners in 2008/09, Shakhtar Donetsk, and the Italian giants Juventus, who were humbled 4-1 at Craven Cottage to give Fulham an unlikely 5-4 aggregate victory. Unfortunately, however, the final against Atletico Madrid proved to be a game too far, with the Spanish side winning 2-1 after extra time. Unfortunately, failure to win the trophy means that European football won't be on offer at Craven Cottage in 2010/11 but fans will be optimistic that the new season will bring a renewed push towards a top six or seven finish. However, Hodgson's departure to take over at Liverpool means some uncertainty with no new manager appointed at the time of writing.

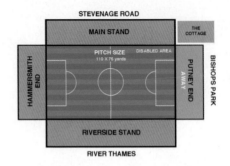

Club Offices: Fulham FC Training Ground, Motspur Park, New Malden, Surrey KT3 6PT
Advance Tickets Tel No: 0870 442 1234
Fax: 020 8442 0236
Training Ground: The Academy, Fulham FC, Motspur Park, New Malden, Surrey, KT3 6PT; Tel: 020 8336 7430
Brief History: Founded in 1879 as St. Andrews Fulham, changed name to Fulham in 1898. Former grounds: Star Road, Ranelagh Club, Lillie Road, Eel Brook Common, Purer's Cross, Barn Elms, Half Moon (Wasps Rugby Football Ground), Craven Cottage (from 1894), moved to Loftus Road 2002 and returned to Craven Cottage for start of the 2004/05 season. Record Attendance: Craven Cottage (49,335)
(Total) Current Capacity: 26,400
Visiting Supporters' Allocation: 3,000 in Putney End
Nearest Railway Station: Putney Bridge (Tube)
Parking (Car): Street parking
Parking (Coach/Bus): Stevenage Road
Police Force and Tel No: Metropolitan (0300 123 1212)
Disabled Visitors' Facilities:
Wheelchairs: Main Stand and Hammersmith End
Blind: No special facility
Anticipated Development(s): It was announced in early October 2008 that the club was looking to increase Craven Cottage's capacity by some 4,000 by infilling the corners between the corners of the existing stands.

◀ 701570
▾ 701581

gillingham

KRBS Priestfield Stadium, Redfern Avenue, Gillingham, Kent, ME7 4DD

website: **WWW.GILLINGHAMFOOTBALLCLUB.COM**
e:mail: **MEDIA@PRIESTFIELD.COM**
tel no: **01634 300000**
colours: **BLUE /WHITE SHIRTS, BLUE SHORTS**
nickname: **THE GILLS**
season 2010/11: **LEAGUE TWO**

Last Season: **21st** (relegated) (p**46**; w**12**; d**14**; l**20**; gf**48**; ga**64**)

Promoted through the Play-Offs at the end of the 2008/09 season, Paul Stimson's Gillingham team were always going to face a challenge in retaining League One status come May 2010. Although the season started brightly with a 5-0 home victory over Swindon Town and a 2-1 win over Plymouth Argyle in the 1st round of the Carling Cup, the team's form was such that a decent run of results was never put together and the club was battling against the drop all season. A run of 10 games – including the 1-0 defeat away at League Two Accrington Stanley in the 3rd round of the FA Cup – from Boxing Day to late February saw the team drift towards the drop zone but the club's fate wasn't ultimately determined until the final Saturday of the season. One of five teams that mathematically could still be relegated – although Orient were pretty safe considering Tranmere's appalling goal difference – a point away at relegated Wycombe would have ensured Gillingham's survival. However, with only six draws and no victories away from home in the League all season, Gillingham probably needed results elsewhere to go in their favour and, for Gills' fans, a 3-0 defeat, combined with victories for both Tranmere and Exeter consigned their team to relegation and an immediate return to League Two. Gillingham's last relegation saw an immediate promotion and it's likely that the team will, once again, be amongst the favourites for the Play-Offs at least in 2010/11. With the season completed, Stimson departed as Gills' boss to be replaced by Andy Hessenthaler, who had previously been boss at Priestfield between 2000 and 2004 and was most recently manager at non-League Dover Athletic.

Advance Tickets Tel No: 01634 300000

Fax: 01634 850986

Training Ground: Beechings Cross, Grange Road, Gillingham ME7 2UD

Brief History: Founded 1893, as New Brompton, changed name to Gillingham in 1913. Founder-members Third Division (1920). Lost Football League status (1938), re-elected to Third Division South (1950). Record attendance 23,002

(Total) Current Capacity: 11,582 (all seated)

Visiting Supporters' Allocation: 1,500 (in Gillingham (Brian Moore Stand) End)

Nearest Railway Station: Gillingham

Parking (Car): Street parking

Parking (Coach/Bus): As directed by Police

Police Force and Tel No: Kent (01622 690690)

Disabled Visitors' Facilities:

Wheelchairs: Redfern Avenue (Main) Stand

Blind: No special facility

Anticipated Development(s): The old open Town End Terrace was demolished during 2003 and replaced by a new temporary open stand. Planning Permission was granted in 2003 for the construction of a new 3,500-seat stand, to be named after noted fan the late Brian Moore, although work has yet to commence. Despite the investment at Priestfield, however, the club is investigating, in conjunction with the local council, the possibility of constructing a new stadium at Temple Marsh. Towards the end of January 2008, chairman Paul Scally announced that he hoped to make a statement about relocation within six weeks with a view to the club moving to a new site within the Medway area but there has been little to report since then.

E   Entrance(s) for visiting
    supporters

1   Gordon Road
2   Priestfield Road
3   Redfern Avenue
4   Gillingham station
    (¼ mile)
5   Gordon Street Stand
6   New two-tier Main
    (Medway) Stand
7   New Rainham End Stand
8   Gillingham End; uncovered
    seating (away)

↑   North direction (approx)

◄ 702840
▼ 702850

hartlepool united

Victoria Park, Clarence Road, Hartlepool, TS24 8BZ

website: **WWW.HARTLEPOOLUNITED.CO.UK**
e:mail: **ENQUIRIES@HARTLEPOOLUNITED.CO.UK**
tel no: **01429 272584**
colours: **BLUE AND WHITE STRIPED SHIRTS, BLUE SHORTS**
nickname: **THE POOLS**
season 2010/11: **LEAGUE ONE**

Last Season: **20th*** (p**46**; w**14**; d**11**; l**21**; gf**59**; ga**67**)

A difficult season for Hartlepool United could have been all the more serious as, having hovered around the drop zone for much of the season, four wins in five matches in April seemed to claw the team away from the drop zone only for the club to be hit with a three-point penalty for having fielded an illegible player in the 2-0 victory over Brighton. As a result, Chris Turner's team faced a tricky last Saturday as one of five teams that could ultimately face relegation to League Two. Fortunately, a 0-0 draw away at Brentford allied to results elsewhere meant that Hartlepool survived irrespective of their appeal against the point deduction. Away from the League, the club had an impressive 1-0 victory away at Championship side Coventry City in the 1st round of the Carling Cup but an embarrassing reverse 1-0 at home to non-League Kettering Town in the 1st round of the FA Cup. For 2010/11, it looks likely that the club will once struggle at the wrong end of the League One table.

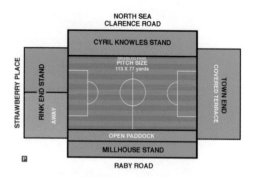

Advance Tickets Tel No: 01429 272584
Fax: 01429 863007
Training Ground: Details omitted at club's request
Brief History: Founded 1908 as Hartlepools United, changed to Hartlepool (1968) and to Hartlepool United in 1977. Founder-members 3rd Division (1921). Record attendance 17,426

(Total) Current Capacity: 7,787 (4,180 seated)
Visiting Supporters' Allocation: 1,000
(located in Rink Stand)

Nearest Railway Station: Hartlepool Church Street
Parking (Car): Street parking and rear of old Clock Garage
Parking (Coach/Bus): As directed
Police Force and Tel No: Cleveland (01642 326326)
Disabled Visitors' Facilities:
Wheelchairs: Cyril Knowles Stand and Rink End
Blind: Commentary available

Anticipated Development(s): The plans for the redevelopment of the Millhouse Stand are still progressing, although there is now no definite timescale. When this work does commence, the ground's capacity will be reduced to 5,000 temporarily.

* Three points deducted as a result of fielding an ineligible player in the match against Brighton on 5 April.

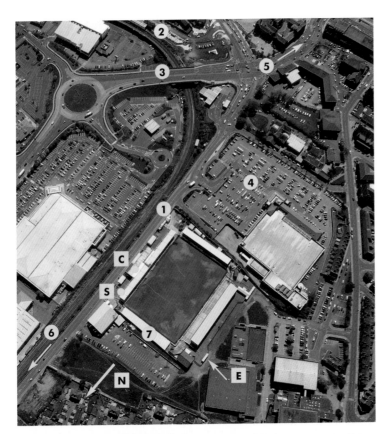

C Club Offices
S Club Shop
E Entrance(s) for visiting
   supporters

1 A179 Clarence Road
2 Hartlepool Church Street
   Station
3 Marina Way
4 Site of former Greyhound
   Stadium
5 To Middlesbrough A689 &
   A1(M)
6 To A19 North
7 Rink End Stand

↑ North direction (approx)

◄ 703176
▼ 703184

hereford united

Edgar Street, Hereford, HR4 9JU

website: **WWW.HEREFORDUNITED.CO.UK**
e:mail: **HUFC1939@HOTMAIL.COM**
tel no: **0844 276 1939**
colours: **WHITE/BLACK SHIRTS, BLACK SHORTS**
nickname: **THE BULLS**
season 2010/11: **LEAGUE TWO**

Last Season: **16th** (p**46**; w**17**; d**8**; l**21**; gf**54**; ga**65**)

Relegated at the end of the 2008/09 season, hopes were high at Edgar Street that the team would make an immediate return to League One. However, a disappointing season saw the Bulls fail to make any serious challenge on the promotion fight and, in early March 2010, John Trewick was dismissed as manager following the 2-0 home defeat against fellow strugglers Macclesfield Town, the team's third home defeat in succession. Trewick, who'd been boss for less than 12 months, was replaced initially by chairman Graham Turner, who thus returned to the managerial dug-out after only a year. He'd previously managed the club for 14 years since replacing John Layton in May 1995. Although the next two games were also lost, seven wins in the club's last 10 matches showed considerable promise for the future. The season, however, ended with some uncertainty as Turner announced in mid-April his willingness to sell his shares in the club as he felt that it required fresh impetus; he subsequently left the club to return to Shrewsbury Town. With new manager Simon Davey at the helm, prospects at Edgar Street in 2010/11 could be bright provided that the form experienced in the last part of the 2009/10 season is replicated.

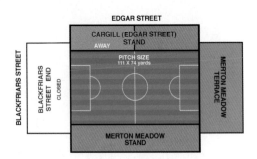

Advance Tickets Tel No: 0844 276 1939
Fax: 0844 276 1982
Training Ground: Details omitted at club's request
Brief History: Founded 1924; first elected to the Football League 1972; relegated to the Conference 1997; promoted through the Play-Offs at the end of 2005/06. Record attendance 18,115
(Total) Current capacity: 5,300; (2,761 seated)
Visiting Supporters' Allocation: In Cargill (Edgar Street) Stand
Nearest Railway Station: Hereford
Parking (Car): Merton Meadow and Edgar Street
Parking (Coach/Bus): Cattle Market
Police Force and Tel No: West Mercia (0300 333 3000)
Disabled Visitors' Facilities:
Wheelchairs: Edgar Street (limited)
Blind: Commentary available
Anticipated Development(s): After some years of deterioration, the Blackfriars Street End was finally closed during the summer of 2009 and this has resulted in the reduction to 5,300 in the ground's total capacity.
On 15 July 2009 the club announced its intention to construct a new 2,000-capacity covered terrace at this end. There is no confirmed timescale for the work.

C Club Offices
S Club Shop
E Entrance(s) for visiting
   supporters
R Refreshment bars for visiting
   supporters
T Toilets for visiting supporters

1 A49(T) Edgar Street
2 Blackfriars Street
3 Cargill (Edgar Street) Stand
4 Merton Meadow Stand
5 Merton Meadow Terrace
6 Blackfriars Street End
   (closed)
7 To Town Centre and
   Hereford station

↑ North direction (approx)

◄ 703018
▼ 703023

huddersfield town

The Galpharm Stadium, Leeds Road, Huddersfield, HD1 6PX

website: **WWW.HTAFC.COM**
e:mail: **INFO@HTAFC.COM**
tel no: **0870 444 4677**
colours: **BLUE AND WHITE STRIPED SHIRTS, WHITE SHORTS**
nickname: **THE TERRIERS**
season 2010/11: **LEAGUE ONE**

Last Season: **6th** (p**46**; w**23**; d**11**; l**12**; gf**82**; ga**56**)

In the hunt for the Play-Offs for the bulk of the season, Lee Clark's Huddersfield Town retained a mathematical – albeit unlikely – chance of snatching the last automatic promotion place right through until the final Saturday of the season. Lying in sixth place with one game left, the Terriers undoubtedly needed results elsewhere to go their way if they were to grab promotion at the end. Facing relegation-threatened Exeter City suggested that Huddersfield had a reasonable chance of taking the victory that might put pressure on the teams above but, in reality, a surprise 2-1 win for the Grecians means that Town remained in sixth place and thus faced Millwall in the Play-Offs. A home draw combined with defeat at the New Den means that Huddersfield will again face League One football in 2010/11 but, with ambitious backing for the manager, the team should certainly be capable of the Play-Offs at least, come May 2011.

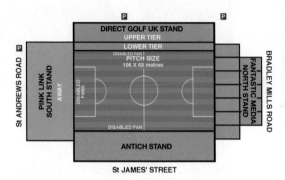

Advance Tickets Tel No: 0870 444 4552
Fax: 01484 484101
Training Ground: Storthes Hall, Storthes Hall Lane, Kirkburton, Huddersfield HD8 0WA
Brief History: Founded 1908, elected to Football League in 1910. First Club to win the Football League Championship three years in succession. Moved from Leeds Road ground to Kirklees (Alfred McAlpine) Stadium 1994/95 season. Record attendance (Leeds Road) 67,037; Galpharm Stadium: 23,678

(Total) Current Capacity: 24,500 (all seated)
Visiting Supporters' Allocation: 4,037 (all seated)
Nearest Railway Station: Huddersfield
Parking (Car): Car parks (pre-sold) adjacent to ground
Parking (Coach/Bus): Car parks adjacent to ground
Other Clubs Sharing Ground: Huddersfield Giants RLFC
Police Force and Tel No: West Yorkshire (0845 606 0606)
Disabled Visitors' Facilities:
Wheelchairs: Three sides of Ground, at low levels and raised area, including toilet access
Blind: Area for partially sighted with Hospital Radio commentary
Anticipated Development(s): With completion of the new North Stand, work on the Galpharm Stadium is over.

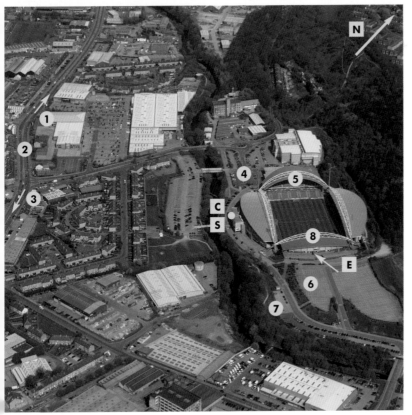

▲ 702224
◀ 702207

C Club Offices
S Club Shop
E Entrance(s) for visiting supporters

1 To Leeds and M62 Junction 25
2 A62 Leeds Road
3 To Huddersfield station (1¼ miles)
4 Disabled parking
5 North Stand
6 St Andrews pay car park
7 Coach park
8 South (Pink Link) Stand (away)

↑ North direction (approx)

hull city

Kingston Communications Stadium, Walton Street, Hull, East Yorkshire, HU3 6HU

website: **WWW.HULLCITYAFC.NET**
e:mail: **INFO@HULLTIGERS.COM**
tel no: **01482 504 600**
colours: **AMBER SHIRTS, BLACK SHORTS**
nickname: **THE TIGERS**
season 2010/11: **CHAMPIONSHIP**

Last Season: **19th** (relegated) (p**38**; w**6**; d**12**; l**20**; gf**34**; ga**75**)

The Tigers were always going to find their second season in the Premier League a struggle, particularly after the rapid descent down the table during the latter part of the 2008/09 season. With the team struggling to make an impact and rooted in the relegation zone, manager Phil Brown was put on gardening leave in mid-March following the home defeat against Arsenal – the club's fourth straight defeat. The club moved quickly to bring in Iain Dowie as new boss until the end of the season, although under the curious title of Football Management Consultant. Unfortunately, Dowie arrival wasn't sufficient to turn the tide as a 1-0 home defeat against Sunderland, following the dispiriting 4-1 home defeat against fellow strugglers Burnley and the 2-0 reverse again at home against Aston Villa, confirmed the Tigers' relegation – barring a goal scoring miracle – back to the Championship. Given the comments made by the chairman, Adam Pearson, about the club's dire financial position, the club's relegation may prove costly. Whilst other teams relegated from the Premier League in recent seasons – most notably West Brom and Burnley – have a secure financial basis to compete at the Championship level, Hull's position looks poor in comparison. There are a number of teams – such as Bradford City and Leeds United – that have lived the Premier League dream only to come crashing down as financial reality kicks in. Given Hull's position the club may well struggle to make an impact in the Championship in 2010/11 and a further relegation cannot be ruled out. New boss Nigel Pearson thus faces a massive challenge.

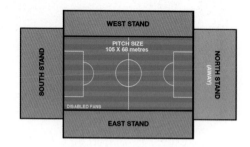

Advance Tickets Tel No: 01482 505 600
Fax: 01482 304882
Training Ground: Millhouse Woods Lane, Cottingham, Kingston upon Hull HU16 4HB
Brief History: Founded 1904. Former grounds: The Boulevard (Hull Rugby League Ground), Dairycoates, Anlaby Road Cricket Circle (Hull Cricket Ground), Anlaby Road, Boothferry Park (from 1946). Moved to Kingston Communications Stadium in late 2002. Record attendance (at Boothferry Park) 55,019; (at Kingston Communications Stadium) 25,512
(Total) Current Capacity: 25,504 (all seated)
Visiting Supporters' Allocation: 2,500 all-seated in North Stand
Nearest Railway Station: Hull Paragon
Parking (Car): There are 1,800 spaces on the Walton Street Fairground for use on match days
Parking (Coach/Bus): As directed
Other Clubs Sharing Ground: Hull RLFC
Police Force and Tel No: Humberside (0845 606 0222)
Disabled Visitors' facilities:
Wheelchairs: c300 places
Blind: Contact club for details
Anticipated Development(s): The club moved into the new Kingston Communication Stadium towards the end of 2002. The ground is shared with Hull RLFC. The total cost of the 25,504-seat ground was £44million. The West Stand is provided with two tiers and there are plans for the construction of a second tier on the East and South Stands, taking the capacity to 34,000, if required.

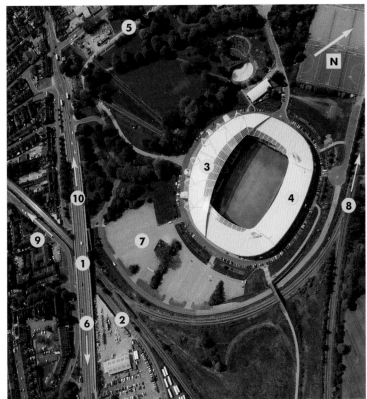

1 A1105 Anlaby Road
2 Arnold Lane
3 West Stand
4 East Stand
5 Walton Street
6 To city centre and railway station
7 Car parks
8 Railway line towards Scarborough
9 Railway line towards Leeds
10 A1105 westwards towards A63 and M62

↑ North direction (approx)

◄ 703188
▼ 703199

ipswich town

Portman Road, Ipswich, IP1 2DA

website: **WWW.ITFC.CO.UK**
e:mail: **ENQUIRIES@ITFC.CO.UK**
tel no: **01473 400500**
colours: **BLUE SHIRTS, WHITE SHORTS**
nickname: **THE TRACTORBOYS**
season 2010/11: **CHAMPIONSHIP**

Last Season: **15th (p46; w12; d20; l14; gf50; ga61)**

With the uncompromising Roy Keane appointed manager towards the end of the 2008/09 season, Ipswich Town were widely regarded as being amongst the favourites for the Play-Offs at least at the beginning of the season. A disastrous start, however, in which the team failed to win a League match until the 1-0 home defeat of Derby County at the end of October, resulted in the Tractor Boys being rooted to the bottom of the League Championship after 15 matches. The poor start to the campaign led to increasing criticism amongst fans of Keane and his tactics but the club persevered and the results started to improve, although it was not until early December that the club started to pull away from the drop zone. Ultimately, the team was to finish in a position of mid-table mediocrity, having won 12 of its last 35 matches and drawn 15. Whilst mid-table is not where the fans expected to be at the start of August, it was a lot better than seemed possible in October and perhaps lays the basis for a more sustained attempt on the Play-Offs for 2010/11.

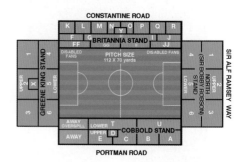

Advance Tickets Tel No: 0870 1110555

Fax: 01473 400040

Training Ground: Ipswich Town Academy, Playford Road, Rushmere, Ipswich IP4 5RU

Brief History: Founded 1887 as Ipswich Association F.C., changed to Ipswich Town in 1888. Former Grounds: Broom Hill & Brookes Hall, moved to Portman Road in 1888. Record attendance 38,010

(Total) Current Capacity: 30,311 (all seated)

Visiting Supporters' Allocation: 1,900 all seated in Cobbold Stand

Nearest Railway Station: Ipswich

Parking (Car): Portman Road, Portman Walk & West End Road

Parking (Coach/Bus): West End Road

Police Force and Tel No: Suffolk (01473 613500)

Disabled Visitors' Facilities:

Wheelchairs: Lower Britannia Stand

Blind: Commentary available

Anticipated Development(s): The new Greene King (South) Stand has been followed by the construction of the new two-tier, 7,035-seat, North Stand, which was initially delayed as a result of legal action. The completion of the two stands takes Portman Road's capacity to more than 30,000. The club has plans, but no timescale, to rebuild the Cobbold Stand to give a capacity of 40,000.

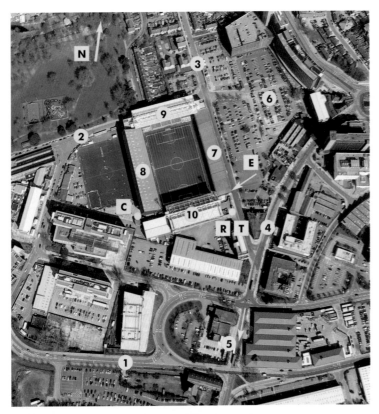

C Club Offices
E Entrance(s) for visiting
  supporters
R Refreshment bars for visiting
  supporters
T Toilets for visiting supporters

1 A137 West End Road
2 Sir Alf Ramsay Way
3 Portman Road
4 Princes Street
5 To Ipswich station
6 Car Parks
7 Cobbold Stand
8 Britannia Stand
9 North (Sir Bobby Robson) Stand
10 Greene King (South) Stand

↑ North direction (approx)

◄ 702854
▼ 702866

leeds united

Elland Road, Leeds, LS11 0ES

website: **WWW.LEEDSUNITED.COM**
e:mail: **RECEPTION@LEEDSUNITED.COM**
tel no: **0871 334 1919**
colours: **WHITE SHIRTS, WHITE SHORTS**
nickname: **THE WHITES**
season 2010/11: **CHAMPIONSHIP**

Last Season: **2nd** (promoted) (p**46**; w**25**; d**11**; l**10**; gf**77**; ga**44**)

Ultimately a season of considerable triumph for Simon Grayson's Leeds United team, with promotion back to the Championship after three seasons in League One alongside claiming the notable scalp of Manchester United in a remarkable 3rd round FA Cup match at Old Trafford. For the Elland Road faithful it was if the great days had returned in a single afternoon. In the League, United started like an express train, not being defeated until the 13th match of the campaign but the second half of the season, almost from the moment the club celebrated its Old Trafford triumph, the wheels seemed to come off; in the first 23 League matches, the club had gained 56 points but in the remaining 23 only 30 points. As a result, the team's fate rested on results on the final day with any one of five teams capable of taking the second automatic promotion place. However, the spot was Leeds's to lose; provided the team defeated Bristol Rovers at home, results elsewhere were immaterial. The team, however, made it hard for themselves, having a player sent off in the first half before going a goal down. Two late goals were, however, sufficient to ensure victory and bring promotion to the Championship. One of the scorers, Jermaine Beckford, had nonetheless played his last game for the club and Grayson will undoubtedly have to strengthen the squad significantly if United are not to struggle in the Championship. As a 'big' team, United ought to be able to bring in players capable of establishing the club in the Championship but consolidation at this new level is perhaps a realistic expectation for 2010/11.

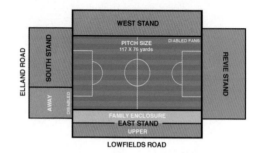

Advance Tickets Tel No: 0871 334 1992
Fax: 0113 367 6050
Training Ground: Thorp Arch, Walton Road, Nr Wetherby LS23 7BA
Brief History: Founded 1919, formed from the former 'Leeds City' club, who were disbanded following expulsion from the Football League in October 1919. Joined Football League in 1920. Record attendance 57,892
(Total) Current Capacity: 40,296 all seated)
Visiting Supporters' Allocation: 1,800 in South East Corner (can be increased to 5,000 in South Stand if necessary)
Nearest Railway Station: Leeds City
Parking (Car): Car parks adjacent to ground
Parking (Coach/Bus): As directed by Police
Police Force and Tel No: West Yorkshire (0113 243 5353)
Disabled Visitors' Facilities:
Wheelchairs: West Stand and South Stand
Blind: Commentary available
Anticipated Development(s): The club announced plans in late 2008 for the construction of a hotel and other facilities behind the East Stand although there is no timescale for the work at present. Elland Road was selected as one of the 12 possible grounds for use in 2018 should England win the World Cup. If the bid proves successful, the ground's capacity would need to be raised to 51,000.

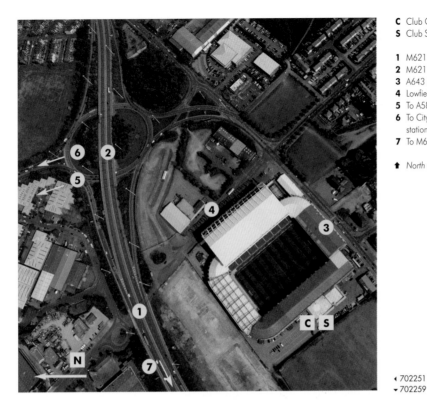

C Club Offices
S Club Shop

1 M621
2 M621 Junction 2
3 A643 Elland Road
4 Lowfields Road
5 To A58
6 To City Centre and
   station
7 To M62 and M1

⬆ *North direction (approx)*

◄ 702251
▼ 702259

leicester city

Walkers Stadium, Filbert Way, Leicester, LE2 7FL

website: **WWW.LCFC.COM**
e:mail: **TICKET.SALES@LCFC.CO.UK**
tel no: **0844 815 6000**
colours: **BLUE SHIRTS, WHITE SHORTS**
nickname: **THE FOXES**
season 2010/11: **CHAMPIONSHIP**

Last Season: **5th** (p**46**; w**21**; d**13**; l**12**; gf**61**; ga**45**)

Promoted as League One champions at the end of the 2008/09 season, Leicester City under Nigel Pearson proved to be one of the surprise packages of the 2009/10 season in the Championship. Whilst never seriously in the hunt for the two automatic promotion places, the club's form throughout the season was sufficient to ensure a Play-Off place with five straight wins in the club's final five League matches. In the Play-Offs the Foxes faced Cardiff City. A 1-0 home defeat combined with a 3-2 win away took the tie to a penalty shoot-out where Cardiff were ultimately to prove triumphant. With two financially-challenged clubs being relegated from the Premier League, 2010/11 represents an excellent chance for clubs such as Leicester to make a serious bid for automatic promotion or the Play-Offs and City should certainly have the potential come the new season to mount a challenge for a top-six finish. However, the club will have to face the challenge of the new season with a new manager – Paulo Sousa from Swansea City – as Pearson left in late June to take over at rivals Hull City.

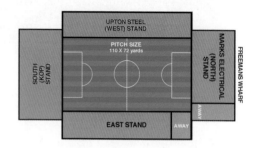

Advance Tickets Tel No: 0844 815 5000
Fax: 0116 247 0585
Training Ground: Middlesex Road, Leicester LE2 8PB
Brief History: Founded 1884 as Leicester Fosse, changed name to Leicester City in 1919. Former grounds: Fosse Road South, Victoria Road, Belgrave Cycle Track, Mill Lane, Aylestone Road Cricket Ground and Filbert Street (from 1891). The club moved to the new Walkers Stadium for the start of the 2002/03 season. Record attendance (at Filbert Street) 47,298; (at Walkers Stadium) 32,148

(Total) Current Capacity: 32,500

Visiting Supporters' Allocation: 3,000 (all seated) in North East of ground

Nearest Railway Station: Leicester

Parking (Car): NCP car park

Parking (Coach/Bus): As directed

Police Force and Tel No: Leicester (0116 222 2222)

Disabled Visitors Facilities:

Wheelchairs: 186 spaces spread through all stands

Blind: Match commentary via hospital radio

Anticipated Developments: The club moved into the new 32,500-seat Walkers Stadium at the start of the 2002/03 season. Although there are no plans at present, the stadium design allows for the construction of a second tier to the East Stand, taking capacity to 40,000.

C Club Offices

1 Raw Dykes Road
2 Freemans Wharf
3 A426 Aylestone Road
4 To Lutterworth
5 To city centre and railway station (one mile)
6 Burnmoor Street to site of former ground
7 River Soar
8 Holiday Inn Express Hotel
9 Marks Electrical (North) Stand
10 East Stand
11 Upton Steel (West) Stand
12 South (Kop) Stand
13 Car Park
14 Filbert Way

⬆ *North direction (approx)*

◄ 702650
▼ 702661

leyton orient

Matchroom Stadium, Brisbane Road, Leyton, London, E10 5NF

website: **WWW.LEYTONORIENT.COM**
e:mail: **INFO@LEYTONORIENT.NET**
tel no: **0871 310 1881**
colours: **RED SHIRTS, RED SHORTS**
nickname: **THE O'S**
season 2010/11: **LEAGUE ONE**

Last Season: **17th** (p**46**; w**13**; d**12**; l**21**; gf**53**; ga**63**)

Easter Saturday was to be a difficult day at Brisbane Road as, following the 3-1 home defeat to Hartlepool, Geraint Williams departed as manager after just over a year as boss. The club's form – only one victory in 11 matches culminating in the reverse against Hartlepool – had resulted in Orient dropping calamitously down the table to the point where the club was only one point above the drop zone. With Kevin Nugent acting as caretaker in the 2-1 defeat at in-form Southampton, chairman Barry Hearn moved quickly to appoint the ex-Yeovil and Brighton boss Russell Slade to the hot-seat. Under Slade, Orient managed to win three and draw one of the club's last six League matches of the season and thus avoid the drop. It was, however a close run thing as the team finished in 17th place, only one point above relegated Gillingham but with a better goal difference than the other two teams – Exeter and Tranmere – that also finished on 51 points. No doubt during the summer, Slade will be keen to rebuild his squad; he's an experienced manager at this level and so, with astute acquisitions, the team could be one of those to watch in 2010/11.

Advance Tickets Tel No: 0871 310 1883

Fax: 0871 310 1882

Training Ground: Southgate Hockey Centre, Trent Park, Snakes Lane, Barnet EN4 0PS

Brief History: Founded 1887 as Clapton Orient, from Eagle Cricket Club (formerly Glyn Cricket Club formed in 1881). Changed name to Leyton Orient (1946), Orient (1966), Leyton Orient (1987). Former grounds: Glyn Road, Whittles Athletic Ground, Millfields Road, Lea Bridge Road, Wembley Stadium (2 games), moved to Brisbane Road in 1937. Record attendance 34,345

(Total) Current Capacity: 9,271 all seated)

Visiting Supporters' Allocation: 1,000 (all seated) in East Stand/Terrace

Nearest Railway Station: Leyton (tube), Leyton Midland Road

Parking (Car): Street parking

Parking (Coach/Bus): As directed by Police

Police Force and Tel No: Metropolitan (0300 123 1212)

Disabled Visitors' Facilities:

Wheelchairs: Windsor Road

Blind: Match commentary supplied on request

Anticipated Development(s): Work was scheduled to start on the North Stand towards the end of October 2006 and the new 1,351-seat structure was completed by the end of the 2006/07 season. In the summer of 2007 plans for the 2012 Olympic Stadium were announced. A permanent capacity of 25,000 is anticipated with a temporary upper tier offering a total capacity of 80,000 for the duration of the Games. There is a possibility, given that no post-2012 use has as yet been identified for the stadium, that Leyton Orient may relocate to the ground for the start of the 2013/14 season.

E Entrance(s) for visiting
supporters

1 Buckingham Road
2 Oliver Road
3 A112 High Road Leyton
4 To Leyton Tube Station
(¼ mile)
5 Brisbane Road
6 Windsor Road
7 To Leyton Midland Road
station
8 South Stand
9 West Stand
10 Main (East) Stand
11 North Stand

↑ *North direction (approx)*

◄ 701472
▼ 701477

lincoln city

Sincil Bank, Lincoln LN5 8LD

website: **WWW.REDIMPS.CO.UK**
e:mail: **LCFC@REDIMPS.COM**
tel no: **01522 880011**
colours: **RED AND WHITE STRIPES, BLACK SHORTS**
nickname: **THE IMPS**
season 2010/11: **LEAGUE TWO**

Last Season: **20th** (p**46**; w**13**; d**11**; l**22**; gf**42**; ga**65**)

In early September, Peter Jackson, who'd been in charge at Sincil Bank for almost two years, was sacked as the Imps' boss following an indifferent start to the campaign that had seen the club win only two of its first five League matches and crash out of both the Carling Cup and Johnstone's Paint Trophy. Simon Clark and Tom Spall were placed in temporary charge until the appointment of Chris Sutton, the well-travelled striker, as new boss in his first managerial role. Under Sutton, the Imps continued to struggle in the League, ultimately finishing just above the drop zone. Manager and fans will be concerned that the club had the worst scoring record of any team in League Two, other than relegated Darlington, and a goal difference that was also amongst the worst in the division. Away from the League, the club managed a reasonable run in the FA Cup – albeit at the expenses of two non-League teams in the guise of Telford United and Northwich Victoria – before crashing out at Premier League Bolton. For the new season, Sutton's priority must be to acquire a proven striker at this level; failure to do so could mean that it's another long and hard season at Sincil Bank.

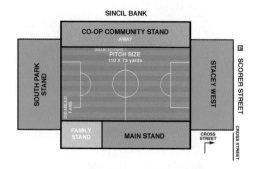

Advance Tickets Tel No: 01522 880011
Fax: 01522 880020
Training Ground: The Sports Ground, Carlton Boulevard, Lincoln LN2 4WJ
Brief History: Founded 1884. Former Ground: John O'Gaunts Ground, moved to Sincil Bank in 1895. Founder-members 2nd Division Football League (1892). Relegated from 4th Division in 1987, promoted from GM Vauxhall Conference in 1988. Record attendance 23,196
(Total) Current Capacity: 10,130 (all seated)
Visiting Supporters' Allocation: 1,900 in Co-op Community Stand (part, remainder for Home fans)
Nearest Railway Station: Lincoln Central
Parking (Car): City centre car parks; limited on-street parking
Parking (Coach/Bus): South Common
Police Force and Tel No: Lincolnshire (0300 111 0300)
Disabled Visitors' Facilities:
Wheelchairs: 72 places behind goals
Blind: No special facility
Anticipated Development(s): Following the replacement of the seats in the Stacey West Stand, Sincil Bank is once again an all-seater stadium.

N

C Club Offices
S Club Shop

1 Family Stand
2 Sincil Bank
3 Sausthorpe Street
4 Cross Street
5 Co-op Community Stand
   (away)
6 A15 South Park Avenue
7 Stacey West Stand
8 Lincoln Central station
   (½ mile)

↑ *North direction (approx)*

◄ 703032
▼ 703034

liverpool

Anfield, Anfield Road, Liverpool L4 0TH

website: **WWW.LIVERPOOLFC.TV**
e:mail: **VIA WEBSITE**
tel no: **0151 263 2361**
colours: **RED SHIRTS, RED SHORTS**
nickname: **THE REDS**
season 2010/11: **PREMIER LEAGUE**

Last Season: **7th (p38; w18; d9; l11; gf61; ga35)**

Was 2009/10 the season in which Liverpool's ambitions to be a top-four club finally exposed as impossible given the current ownership? One of a number of clubs where questions of ownership and funding were brought into sharp relief, Liverpool's challenge for the Premier League title disappeared almost as soon as the season started. There were freak results – most notably the beach ball assisting Sunderland to a 1-0 victory at the Stadium of Light — but little could disguise the fact that, with the loss of Alonso in the close season, the team was increasingly reliant on two players – Torres and Gerrard – both of who were prone to injury. Failure to progress from the group stage of the Champions League allied to defeat in the Europa League semi-final were disappointing whilst the team also failed to make significant progress in the domestic cup competitions. Finishing in seventh at least ensures entry to the Europa League in 2010/11 but not the riches offered by the Champions League. With uncertainty following the departure of manager Rafael Benitez and possibly of key players, plus the limited funds available to strengthen the squad, it looks unlikely that Liverpool will be able to achieve much more in 2010/11 given the funding available to ambitious teams like Manchester City. At the end of June it was announced that the experienced Roy Hodgson was to be the club's new manager. He faces a great challenge in not only retaining players but restoring Liverpool's fortunes.

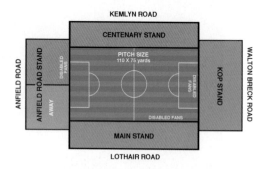

Advance Tickets Tel No: 0870 220 2345

Fax: 0151 260 8813

Ticket Enquiries Fax: 0151 261 1416

Training Ground: Melwood Drive, West Derby, Liverpool L12 8SV; Tel: 0151 282 8888

Brief History: Founded 1892. Anfield Ground formerly Everton F.C. Ground. Joined Football League in 1893. Record attendance 61,905

(Total) Current Capacity: 45,362 all seated)

Visiting Supporters' Allocation: 1,972 (all seated) in Anfield Road Stand

Nearest Railway Station: Kirkdale

Parking (Car): Stanley car park

Parking (Coach/Bus): Priory Road and Pinehurst Avenue

Police Force and Tel No: Merseyside (0151 709 6010)

Disabled Visitors' Facilities:

Wheelchairs: Kop and Main Stands

Blind: Commentary available

Anticipated Development(s): Full planning permission was granted in June 2008 for the construction of the 60,000-seat stadium at Stanley Park. The design allows for the capacity to be increased to 73,000 if required. Original plans envisaged the ground being completed for the start of the 2011/12 season but it was announced in late 2008 that the club was delaying construction for at least 12 months as a result of the credit crunch and the loss of funds from the European Regional Development Fund that had originally been allocated for the regeneration of the Anfield area.

N

C Club Offices
S Club Shop

1 Car Park
2 Anfield Road
3 A5089 Walton Breck Road
4 Kemlyn Road
5 Kirkdale station
  (1 mile)
6 Utting Avenue
7 Stanley Park
8 Spion Kop
9 Anfield Road Stand

↑ North direction (approx)

◄ 702114
▼ 702108

macclesfield town

Moss Rose Ground, London Road, Macclesfield, SK11 7SP

website: **WWW.MTFC.CO.UK**
e:mail: **OFFICE@MTFC.CO.UK**
tel no: **01625 264686**
colours: **ROYAL BLUE SHIRTS, WHITE SHORTS**
nickname: **THE SILKMEN**
season 2010/11: **LEAGUE TWO**

Last Season: **19th** (p**46**; w**12**; d**18**; l**16**; gf**49**; ga**58**)

Although the Silkmen ultimately achieved a position of mid-table safety, for fans of the club and for football fans throughout the country, the 2009/10-season will always be overshadowed by the sad death of Keith Alexander at the tragically young age of 53. Well-liked and popular, Alexander, who'd been boss at Moss Rose since February 2008, had had a history of ill health before he collapsed and died in early March following the team's 1-0 defeat at Notts County. He was replaced as caretaker boss by assistant Gary Simpson, who, after a run of 18 points from 10 games, was confirmed as the permanent manager in mid-April. Provided that the Silkmen maintain the same progress in 2010/11, the team might have the potential for a top-half finish.

A523 LONDON ROAD

Advance Tickets Tel No: 01625 264686
Fax: 01625 264692
Training Ground: Details omitted at club's request
Brief History: Founded 1874. Previous ground: Rostron Field moved to Moss Rose Ground in 1891. Winners of the Vauxhall Conference in 1994/95 and 1996/97. Admitted to Football League for 1997/98 season. Record attendance 10,041
(Total) Current Capacity: 6,335; (2,599 seated)
Visiting Supporters' Allocation: 1,900 (1,500 in Silkman Terrace; 400 seated in Estate Road Stand)
Nearest Railway Station: Macclesfield
Parking (Car): No parking at the ground and the nearest off-street car park is in the town centre (25min walk). There is some on-street parking in the vicinity, but this can get crowded.
Parking (Coach/Bus): As directed
Police Force and Tel No: Cheshire (0845 458 0000)
Disabled Visitors' Facilities:
Wheelchairs: 45 places in Estate Road Stand
Blind: No special facility
Anticipated Development(s): In early December 2009 the club's Chief Executive announced that there was a possibility that the club would relocate given that Moss Rose was ageing and difficult to redevelop. If the club did move, it would seek a site close to the town centre. There is, however, nothing as yet confirmed.

C Club Offices
E Entrance(s) for visiting
supporters

1 A523 London Road
2 To Town Centre and station
(1.5 miles)
3 To Leek
4 Moss Lane
5 Star Lane
6 Site of Silkmans Public
House (now demolished)
7 Star Lane End
8 Silkman End (away section)
9 Estate Road Stand

↑ North direction (approx)

◄ 703224
▼ 703228

manchester city

The City of Manchester Stadium, Sportcity, Manchester M11 3FF

website: **WWW.MCFC.CO.UK**
e:mail: **MCFC@MCFC.CO.UK**
tel no: **0870 062 1894**
colours: **SKY BLUE SHIRTS, WHITE SHORTS**
nickname: **THE BLUES**
season 2010/11: **PREMIER LEAGUE**

Last Season: **5th** (p**38**; w**18**; d**13**; l**7**; gf**73**; ga**45**)

Owned since 2008 by Middle Eastern interests, whose ambitions for the club seem almost as unlimited as their wealth, Manchester City now find themselves portrayed as the wealthiest club in Britain. During the close season in 2009 Mark Hughes made a number of significant additions to the squad and the team was undoubtedly predicated on breaking the monopoly of the top-four places by Arsenal, Chelsea, Liverpool and Manchester United. Hughes's position was reliant upon being seen to bring Champions League football to the City of Manchester Stadium. However, following the 3-0 defeat away at Tottenham Hotspur, a result that left the club in eighth position, Hughes was sacked in mid-December and immediately replaced by the Italian Roberto Mancini. Initially, results under Mancini suggested that the club could secure a place in the top four with some ease but for much of the second half of the season the team's form was too inconsistent – a 4-2 victory at Stamford Bridge, for example, alongside a 2-1 defeat away at Hull City – to tie-up the all-important fourth place. It was, however, not until the 1-0 home defeat by Tottenham Hotspur in the penultimate League match, a result that ensured that the Londoners would finish fourth, that meant that the team would have to endure the Europa rather than Champions League. Away from the League, City had a good run in the Carling Cup, before being beaten in the semi-finals by Manchester United. For 2010/11, the challenge for Mancini is the same as that for Hughes at the start of the previous season: create a team capable of taking a place in the top four. With the financial resources at his disposal, Mancini ought to be able to achieve this and the team may, perhaps, threaten to go further and challenge for the title.

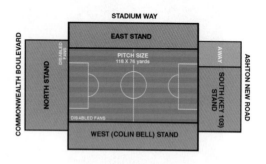

Advance Tickets Tel No: 0870 062 1894
Fax: 0161 438 7999
Training Ground: Platt Lane Complex, Yew Tree Road, Fallowfield, Manchester M14 7UU;
Tel: 0161 248 6610; Fax: 0161 257 0030
Brief History: Founded 1880 at West Gorton, changed name to Ardwick (reformed 1887) and to Manchester City in 1894. Former grounds: Clowes Street (1880-81), Kirkmanshulme Cricket Club (1881-82), Queens Road (1882-84), Pink Bank Lane (1884-87), Hyde Road (1887-1923) and Maine Road (from 1923 until 2003). Moved to the City of Manchester Stadium for the start of the 2003/04 season. Founder-members 2nd Division (1892). Record attendance (at Maine Road) 84,569 (record for a Football League Ground); at City of Manchester Stadium 47,726
(Total) Current Capacity: 48,000 (all seated)
Visiting Supporters' Allocation: 3,000 (South Stand); can be increased to 4,500 if required
Nearest Railway Station: Manchester Piccadilly
Parking (Car): Ample match day parking available to the north of the stadium, entrance via Alan Turing Way. On-street parking restrictions operate in all areas adjacent to the stadium on matchdays.
Parking (Coach/Bus): Coach parking for visiting supporters is adjacent to turnstiles at Key 103 Stand. For home supporters to the north of the stadium, entrance from Alan Turing Way.
Police Force and Tel No: Greater Manchester (0161 872 5050)
Disabled Visitors' facilities:
Wheelchairs: 300 disabled seats around ground
Blind: 14 places alongside helpers in East Stand Level 1. Commentary available via headsets.

1 A662 Ashton New Road
2 Commonwealth Boulevard
3 Stadium Way
4 A6010 Alan Turing Way
5 North Stand
6 South (Key 103) Stand
7 West (Colin Bell) Stand
8 East Stand
9 National Squash Centre
10 Warm-up track
11 To Manchester city centre
   and Piccadilly station
   (1¹/₂ miles)

↑ North direction (approx)

◄ 701776
▼ 701787

manchester united

Old Trafford, Sir Matt Busby Way, Manchester, M16 0RA

website: **WWW.MANUTD.COM**
e:mail: **ENQUIRIES@MANUTD.CO.UK**
tel no: **0161 868 8000**
colours: **RED SHIRTS, WHITE SHORTS**
nickname: **THE RED DEVILS**
season 2010/11: **PREMIER LEAGUE**

Last Season: **2nd** (p**38**; w**27**; d**4**; l**7**; gf**86**; ga**28**)

A disappointing season on the field, with only the Carling Cup to show for the team's endeavours and a worrying one off it with growing concerns about the financial implications of the club's ownership by the Glazer family, 2009/10 will perhaps be a season that many Manchester United fans would prefer to forget. The rise of the 'green and yellow' protest movement and the interest engendered by the possible take-over of the club by the Red Knights are symptomatic of a club that seems to have lost its way amongst its loyal supporters. On the field, the Premier League was pretty much a two-horse race throughout the season, between United and Chelsea, although Arsenal did threaten on occasions. The 2-1 home defeat by Chelsea gave the Londoners the edge but it was not until the final Sunday of the season that Chelsea's triumph was confirmed. Although United beat Stoke 4-0, Chelsea's 8-0 thrashing of Wigan ensured that United would finish second. In the Champions League, United progressed reasonably comfortably until the quarter-finals when United went out to Bayern Munich 4-4 on the away goals rule, having initially lost 2-1 in Germany and winning 3-2 at Old Trafford. The loss of Ronaldo in the 2009 close season was perhaps a major factor, as it placed a greater reliance on Rooney. For the new season, Ferguson will undoubtedly be looking to strengthen the squad, although how far he is constrained by the club's financial position is difficult to ascertain. The squad will need additional quality if it is to thrive on both domestic and international fronts and, whilst the team will always be one of those vying for the title, the rise of well-funded City and the increasing dominance of Spanish clubs in European competition mean that silverware could be even harder to achieve in 2010/11 than in 2009/10.

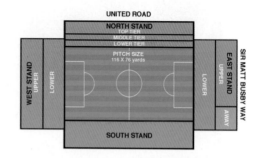

Advance Tickets Tel No: 0161 868 8000
Fax: 0161 868 8804
Training Ground: Carrington Training Complex, Birch Road, Manchester M31 4HH
Brief History: Founded in 1878 as 'Newton Heath L&Y', later Newton Heath, changed to Manchester United in 1902. Former Grounds: North Road, Monsall & Bank Street, Clayton, moved to Old Trafford in 1910 (used Manchester City F.C. Ground 1941-49). Founder-members Second Division (1892). Record attendance 76,962
(Total) Current Capacity: 76,100 (all seated)
Visiting Supporters' Allocation: Approx. 3,000 in corner of South and East Stands
Nearest Railway Station: At Ground
Parking (Car): Lancashire Cricket Ground and White City
Parking (Coach/Bus): As directed by Police
Police Force and Tel No: Greater Manchester (0161 872 5050)
Disabled Visitors' Facilities:
Wheelchairs: South East Stand
Blind: Commentary available
Anticipated Development(s): The work on the £45 million project to construct infills at the north-east and north-west corners of the ground has now been completed and takes Old Trafford's capacity to 76,000, making it by some margin the largest league ground in Britain. Any future development of the ground will involve the Main (South) Stand although work here is complicated by the proximity of the building to the adjacent railway line.

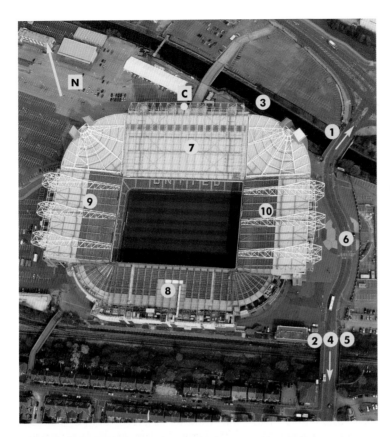

C Club Offices

1 To A5081 Trafford Park Road to M63 Junction 4 (5 miles)
2 A56 Chester Road
3 Bridgewater Canal
4 To Old Trafford Cricket Ground
5 To Parking and Warwick Road station
6 Sir Matt Busby Way
7 North Stand
8 South Stand
9 West Stand
10 East Stand

↑ *North direction (approx)*

◄ 701060
▼ 701063

middlesbrough

Riverside Stadium, Middlesbrough, Cleveland TS3 6RS

website: **WWW.MFC.CO.UK**
e:mail: **ENQUIRIES@MFC.CO.UK**
tel no: **0844 499 6789**
colours: **RED SHIRTS, WHITE SHORTS**
nickname: **BORO**
season 2010/11: **CHAMPIONSHIP**

Last Season: **11th** (p**46**; w**16**; d**14**; l**16**; gf**58**; ga**50**)

Relegated at the end of the 2008/09 season, Boro' were widely expected to be amongst the teams pushing for either automatic promotion or, at worst, the Play-Offs. Like Newcastle United and West Brom, the other two teams relegated, Gareth Southgate's team made a reasonable start to the new season and so it came as a bit of a surprise when, at the end of October, the manager was sacked following the 2-0 victory over Derby County – a result that left Boro' in fourth place in the Championship. Having sacked Southgate after 13 League matches, chairman Steve Gibson moved quickly to appoint Gordon Strachan, recently departed as manager of Celtic, to the vacancy. However, if the tactic was to ensure a swift return to Premier League football, it was sadly misplaced as the team's performances worsened and an inexorable decline down the Championship table ensued. Thus both the Play-Offs and automatic promotion were missed and so Boro' face a second season in the Championship. Given that the club's parachute payments cease at the end of 2010/11, this is probably the team's best opportunity to make a return to the top flight, particularly as the three relegated teams are not the strongest that might have been relegated from the Premier League. Anything short of the Play-Offs will be a disaster for fans and, potentially, for the club.

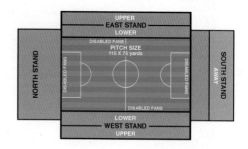

Advance Tickets Tel No: 0844 499 1234
Fax: 01642 757697
Training Ground: Rockcliffe Park, Hurworth Place, Near Darlington, County Durham DL2 2DU; Tel: 01325 722222
Brief History: Founded 1876. Former Grounds: Archery Ground (Albert Park), Breckon Hill Road, Linthorpe Road, moved to Ayresome Park in 1903, and to current ground in Summer 1995. F.A. Amateur Cup winners 1894 and 1897 (joined Football League in 1899). Record attendance (Ayresome Park) 53,596, (Riverside Stadium) 35,000
(Total) Current Capacity: 35,100 (all seated)
Visiting Supporters' Allocation: 4,500 maximum (in the South Stand)
Nearest Railway Station: Middlesbrough
Parking (Car): All parking at stadium is for permit holders
Parking (Coach/Bus): As directed
Police Force and Tel No: Cleveland (01642 326326)
Disabled Visitors' Facilities:
Wheelchairs: More than 170 places available for disabled fans
Blind: Commentary available
Anticipated Development(s): There remain long-term plans for the ground's capacity to be increased to 42,000 through the construction of extra tiers on the North, South and East stands, although there is no confirmed timetable for this work at the current time.

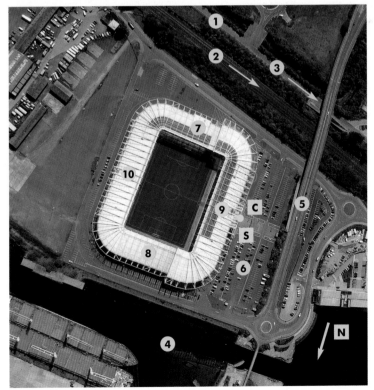

▲ 703281
◀ 703272

C Club Offices
S Club Shop

1 Cargo Fleet Road
2 To Middlesbrough
railway station
3 To Middlesbrough
town centre
4 Middlesbrough Docks
5 Shepherdson Way to A66
6 Car parks
7 South Stand (away)
8 North Stand
9 West Stand
10 East Stand

↑ *North direction (approx)*

millwall

The Den, Zampa Road, London, SE16 3LN

website: **WWW.MILLWALLFC.CO.UK**
e:mail: **QUESTIONS@MILLWALLPLC.COM**
tel no: **020 7232 1222**
colours: **BLUE SHIRTS, WHITE SHORTS**
nickname: **THE LIONS**
season 2010/11: **CHAMPIONSHIP**

Last Season: **3rd** (promoted) (p**46**; w**24**; d**13**; l**9**; gf**76**; ga**44**)

Although the season started slowly, it wasn't long before Kenny Jackett's Millwall team found their stride in League One. The club gradually mounted a sustained campaign to take one of the two automatic promotion spots although it took a dramatic loss of form by Leeds United in the second half of the season to open up the promotion race. Ultimately, Millwall was one of five teams with a mathematical chance of talking second spot in the division come the final Saturday of the season; of the five, Millwall faced rivals Swindon Town at home knowing that the team had to better the result from Elland Road – where Leeds were playing Bristol Rovers – to pip the West Yorkshire team. In the event, Leeds' home victory rendered Millwall's home victory meaningless and consigned the London team to the Play-Offs. A 2-0 aggregate victory over Huddersfield Town set up a Wembley final ironically against Swindon and a further victory – this time 1-0 – was enough to send Millwall up to the Championship. The club's first priority in 2010/11 will be to establish itself at this higher level but a position mid-table come May 2011 is a distinct possibility.

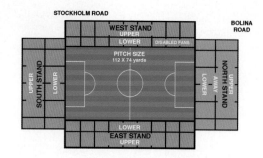

Advance Tickets Tel No: 020 7231 9999

Fax: 020 7231 3663

Training Ground: Millwall FC Training Ground, Calmont Road (off Ashgrove Road), Bromley Hill, Bromley, Kent BR1 4BZ

Brief History: Founded 1885 as Millwall Rovers, changed name to Millwall Athletic (1889) and Millwall (1925). Former Grounds: Glengall Road, East Ferry Road (two separate Grounds), North Greenwich Ground and The Den – Cold Blow Lane – moved to New Den 1993/94 season. Founder-members Third Division (1920). Record attendance: (at The Den) 48,672; (at New Den) 20,093

(Total) Current Capacity: 20,150 (all seated)

Visiting Supporters' Allocation: 4,000 in North Stand

Nearest Railway Station: South Bermondsey or Surrey Quays

Parking (Car): Juno Way car parking (8 mins walk)

Parking (Coach/Bus): At Ground

Police Force and Tel No: Metropolitan (0300 123 1212)

Disabled Visitors' Facilities:

Wheelchairs: 200 spaces in West Stand Lower Tier

Blind: Commentary available

C Club Offices
S Club Shop
E Entrance(s) for visiting
   supporters

1 Bolina Road
2 South Bermondsey station
3 Footpath to station for away
   fans
4 Zampa Road
5 Stockholm Road
6 North Stand (away)

↑ North direction (approx)

◀ 701493
▾ 701509

milton keynes dons

Stadium: MK, Stadium Way West, Milton Keynes, MK1 1ST

website: **WWW.MKDONS.COM**
e:mail: **INFO@MKDONS.COM**
tel no: **01908 622922**
colours: **WHITE/BLACK SHIRTS, WHITE SHORTS**
nickname: **THE DONS**
season 2010/11: **LEAGUE ONE**

Last Season: **12th** (p**46**; w**17**; d**9**; l**20**; gf**60**; ga**68**)

In a season when Milton Keynes Dons were widely expected to feature in the battle for the Play-Offs at the very least, the campaign started well for Paul Ince's team with the Play-Offs a distinct possibility. However, a dramatic decline in form that saw the team win none of the final 11 League matches saw the club drift into a position of mid-table mediocrity. In the middle of April, Paul Ince announced that he intended to stand down as Dons' boss at the end of the season, citing a reduction in the budget for 2010/11 as one of the causes. Having spent heavily in 2009/10 in order to try and secure promotion, the tightened budget at Stadium: MK probably means that the new manager – Karl Robinson – will perhaps struggle and probably means that a top-half finish is the best that fans can hope for.

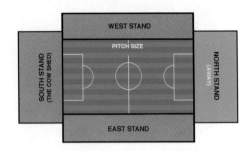

Advance Tickets Tel No: 01908 622900
Fax: 01908 622933
Training Ground: Woughton on the Green, Milton Keynes
Brief History: Founded 1889 as Wimbledon Old Centrals, changed name to Wimbledon in 1905 and to Milton Keynes Dons in 2004. Former grounds: Wimbledon Common, Pepy's Road, Grand Drive, Merton Hall Road, Malden Wanderers Cricket Ground, Plough Lane, Selhurst Park (1991-2002) and National Hockey Stadium (2002-2007); moved to Stadium: MK for start of the 2007/08 season. Elected to the Football League in 1977. Record attendance (Plough Lane) 18,000; (Selhurst Park) 30,115; (National Hockey Stadium) 5,306; (Stadium: MK) 20,222
(Total) Current Capacity: 22,000 (all seated)
Visiting Supporters' Allocation: c3000 in northeast corner
Nearest Railway Station: Bletchley (two miles); Milton Keynes Central (four miles)
Parking (Car): The ground is located within a retail development and parking restrictions at the ground will probably apply.
Parking (Coach/Bus): As directed
Police Force and Tel No: Thames Valley Police (0845 850 5505)
Disabled Visitors' Facilities:
Wheelchairs: 164 spaces
Blind: No special facility
Anticipated Development(s): Following a number of years at the National Hockey Stadium, the Milton Keynes Dons moved into the new Stadium: MK for the start of the 2007/08 season. The ground has been designed to facilitate the addition of a second tier of seating if required in the future, taking the total capacity to 30,000. Stadium: MK was selected as one of the 12 possible grounds for use in 2018 should England host the World Cup. If the bid proves successful, the ground's capacity would need to be raised to 44,000.

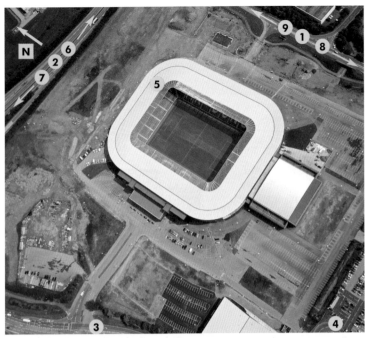

1 B4034 Saxon Street
2 A5
3 Grafton Street
4 Bletcham Way
5 Away Area
6 A5 Southbound to London
7 A5 Northbound to Milton
   Keynes centre and Towcester
8 To Bletchley railway station
   (two miles)
9 To Milton Keynes Central
   railway station (four miles)

↑ North direction (approx)

◄ 702717
▼ 702730

morecambe

The Globe Arena, Christie Way, Morecambe LA4 4TB

website: **WWW.MORECAMBEFC.COM**
e:mail: **OFFICE@MORECAMBEFC.COM**
tel no: **01524 411797***
colours: **RED SHIRTS, WHITE SHORTS**
nickname: **SHRIMPS**
season 2010/11: **LEAGUE TWO**

Last Season: **4th** (p**46**; w**20**; d**13**; l**13**; gf**73**; ga**64**)

In Morecambe's final season at its old Christie Park ground, the season started abysmally for Sammy McIlroy's team as the side went without a single win in its first seven League matches and also crashed out of the Carling Cup 5-1 at Preston North End. Even after 14 matches, the team had only managed to gain a single victory and it looked as though the club would be battling to avoid the drop rather than be interested in the promotion campaign. However, a run of seven wins in nine matches from late October saw the Shrimps gradually move up the League Two table but it was not until the final few weeks of the season that a Play-Off place looked possible. Victory in the final League match at Christie Park, 1-0 over promotion rivals Aldershot Town, ensured a top-seven finish and set up a Play-Off semi-final against Dagenham & Redbridge. However, a 6-0 defeat in London meant that the tie was beyond McIlroy's team despite a 2-1 victory in the last ever match at Christie Park. With the buzz that the move will engender, plus the optimism wrought by performances in the later stages of the 2009/10 season, Morecambe should certainly have the potential to be serious contenders for the Play-Offs again in 2010/11.

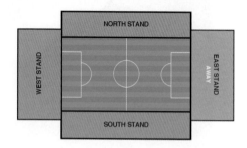

Advance Tickets Tel No: 01524 411797*
Fax: 01524 832230*
Training Ground: Address omitted at club's request
Brief History: 1920. Previous grounds: Morecambe Cricket Ground; moved to Roseberry Park 1921; ground later renamed Christie Park after the club's president who had funded its purchase; moved to new ground for start of the 2010/11 season. Joined Conference at the end of the 1995/96 season and promoted to the Football League at the end of the 2006/07 season. Record attendance (at Christie Park) 9,234
(Total) Current Capacity: 6,476 (2,247 seats)
Visiting Supporters' Allocation: 1,389 on East Stand (standing)
Nearest Railway Station: Morecambe
Parking (Car): As directed
Parking (Coach/Bus): As directed
Police Force and Tel No: Lancashire Constabulary (0845 125 3545)
Disabled Visitors' Facilities:
Wheelchairs: tbc
Blind: tbc
Anticipated Development(s): Work commenced on the construction of the club's new £12 million ground at Westgate on 10 August 2009. The new ground's capacity will be 6,476 including a main stand seating 2,173, a home stand for 2,234 standing fans, an away stand with a capacity of 1,389 standing and a covered terrace of 606.

*These are the numbers for Christie Park and may change with the relocation (although the club has indicated that it intends to retain the existing numbers)

1 Westgate
2 Railway to Morecambe
  station
3 To A589
4 To A589 Marine Road West
  and sea front
5 Acre Moss Lane
6 Westcliffe Drive
7 To railway station
8 Railway to Liverpool

⬆ *North direction (approx)*

◀ 703284
▼ 703295

newcastle united

Sportsdirect.com@St James' Park, Newcastle-upon-Tyne, NE1 4ST

website: **WWW.NUFC.CO.UK**
e:mail: **CONTACT VIA WEBSITE**
tel no: **0844 372 1892**
colours: **BLACK AND WHITE STRIPED SHIRTS, BLACK SHORTS**
nickname: **THE MAGPIES**
season 2010/11: **PREMIER LEAGUE**

Last Season: **1st** (promoted) (p**46**; w**30**; d**12**; l**4**; gf**90**; ga**35**)

Relegated from the Premier League at the end of 2008/09, things looked grim for the Magpies during the close season with no new management appointee following the departure of Alan Shearer, the club up for sale and a 6-1 defeat in a pre-season friendly at Leyton Orient. However, under Chris Hughton, the team performed well in the Championship and achieved promotion back to the Premier League over the Easter weekend. Whilst the Toon's triumph will undoubtedly restore one of the biggest teams in England to the Premier League, many of the fundamental problems afflicting the club – in particular uncertainty over the club's future ownership – must make fans concerned about survival in the Premier League. At the time of writing Hughton remains in charge; it remains to be seen whether the club's promotion will see a higher profile boss brought in. However, given that promotion was achieved largely with the squad that failed to survive in 2008/09, there must be serious doubts as to whether the club can make a serious stab at Premier League survival without significant investment in the squad.

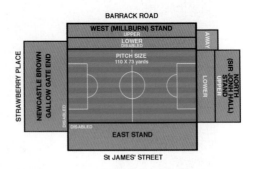

Advance Tickets Tel No: 0844 372 1892
Fax: 0191 201 8600
Training Ground: Darsley Park, Whitley Road, Benton, Newcastle upon Tyne NE12 9FA
Brief History: Founded in 1882 as Newcastle East End, changed to Newcastle United in 1892. Former Grounds: Chillingham Road, moved to St. James' Park (former home of defunct Newcastle West End) in 1892. Record attendance 68,386
(Total) Current Capacity: 52,387 (all seated)
Visiting Supporters' Allocation: 3,000 in North West Stand
Nearest Railway Station: Newcastle Central
Parking (Car): Leazes car park and street parking
Parking (Coach/Bus): Leazes car park
Police Force and Tel No: Northumbria (0345 604 3043)
Disabled Visitors' Facilities:
Wheelchairs: 103 spaces available
Blind: Commentary available
Anticipated Development(s): The club announced plans in March 2007 for a £300 million scheme to increase capacity at St James' Park to 60,000. The work, which would include the construction of a hotel and conference city, will see the expansion of the Gallowgate End.
The project, which has yet to receive planning consent, has no confirmed timescale at present.

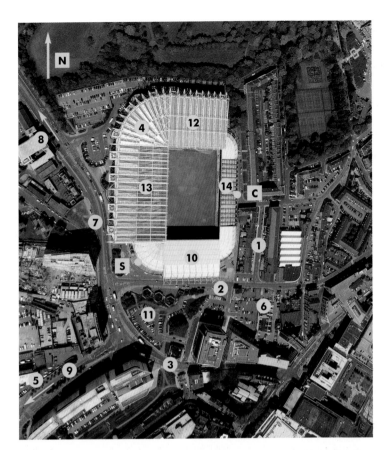

C Club Offices
S Club Shop

1 St. James's Park
2 Strawberry Place
3 Gallowgate
4 Away Section
5 To Newcastle Central station
($\frac{1}{2}$ mile) & A6127(M)
6 Car Park
7 Barrack Road (A189)
8 To A1 and North
9 Corporation Street
10 Gallowgate End
11 Metro Station
12 Sir John Hall Stand
13 Millburn Stand
14 East Stand

↑ North direction (approx)

◀ 703248
▼ 703259

northampton town

Sixfields Stadium, Northampton, NN5 5QA

website: **WWW.NTFC.CO.UK**
e:mail: **GARETH.WILSHIRE@NTFC.TV**
tel no: **01604 683700**
colours: **CLARET SHIRTS, WHITE SHORTS**
nickname: **THE COBBLERS**
season 2010/11: **LEAGUE TWO**

Last Season: **10th** (p**46**; w**18**; d**13**; l**15**; gf**62**; ga**53**)

A disappointing season for the Cobblers following their relegation at the end of the 2008/09 season as many believed that the team would be amongst the favourites to make the Play-Offs at least. A poor start to the campaign saw Stuart Gray depart as manager in early September after nine matches with the team languishing in 16th place. The club moved quickly to appoint Ian Sampson as caretaker-boss and he was named manager for the remainder of the season in early October. Thereafter form was patchy but a run of six runs and a draw took the team up to fifth place in the table in early April and suggested that the Play-Offs were by no means an impossibility. However, a run then of a single win and two draws in the club's final seven League matches saw the team miss out on the Play-Offs. For the new season, Town ought again to be one of the teams capable of reaching the Play-Offs but again a top-half finish is perhaps the best that can be expected.

Advance Tickets Tel No: 01604 683777
Fax: 01604 751613
Training Ground: Adjacent to main ground
Brief History: Founded 1897. Former, County, Ground was part of Northamptonshire County Cricket Ground. Moved to Sixfields Stadium during early 1994/95 season. Record attendance 24,523 (at County Ground); 7,557 (at Sixfields)

(Total) Current Capacity: 7,653 (all seated)
Visiting Supporters' Allocation: 800 (in Paul Cox Panel and Paint South Stand)
Nearest Railway Station: Northampton
Parking (Car): Adjacent to Ground
Parking (Coach/Bus): Adjacent to Ground
Police Force and Tel No: Northants (0300 011 1222)
Disabled Visitors' Facilities:
Wheelchairs: Available on all four sides
Blind: Available

Anticipated Development(s): In early August 2009 it was confirmed that the club and Borough Council were to progress plans for the development of Sixfields. Following further development work, it was expected that a planning application would be lodged with the council in late 2009. The intention is to increase capacity to 15,000.

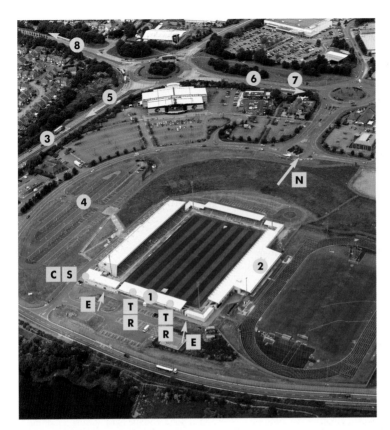

C Club Offices
S Club Shop
E Entrance(s) for visiting
   supporters
R Refreshment bars for visiting
   supporters
T Toilets for visiting supporters

1 South Stand (away)
2 Athletics Stand (double-sided
   stand backs on th the East
   Stand)
3 Upton Way
4 Car parks
5 A45 towards A43
   (Towcester and A5)
6 Weedon Road
7 To Town Centre and station
8 A45 to M1 (Jct 16)

↑ North direction (approx)

◄ 702744
▼ 702750

norwich city

Carrow Road, Norwich, NR1 1JE

website: **WWW.CANARIES.CO.UK**
e:mail: **RECEPTION@NCFC-CANARIES.CO.UK**
tel no: **01603 760760**
colours: **YELLOW SHIRTS, GREEN SHORTS**
nickname: **THE CANARIES**
season 2010/11: **CHAMPIONSHIP**

Last Season: **1st** (promoted) (p**46**; w**29**; d**8**; l**9**; gf**89**; ga**47**)

Relegated from the Championship at the end of the 2008/09 season, the new campaign started disastrously for the Canaries as, in the first game of the season, the team was trounced 7-1 at Carrow Road by local rivals Colchester United. City's worst ever home defeat was to bring a swift end to Bryan Gunn's managerial presence as he was sacked the following week despite overseeing the club's victory away at Swindon in the First Round of the Carling Cup. The club moved quickly to appoint Paul Lambert – ironically previously the boss at Colchester – to the position. Under Lambert the team initially continued to struggle although form gradually picked up and the team gradually closed in on the Play-Off places. However, a run of eight straight wins in December and January – including a 5-0 revenge thrashing of Colchester United – took the Canaries into the automatic promotion places and promotion back to the Championship at the first attempt was secured following the 1-0 victory away at Play-Off chasing Charlton Athletic. Free-scoring City, with Grant Holt to the fore, ought to be capable of at least a mid-table position in the Championship in 2010/11 although the major concern might be that, given Lambert's success, the manager might be tempted to move if a larger club came along.

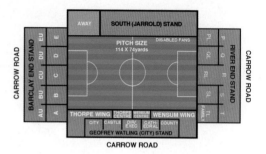

CARROW ROAD

Advance Tickets Tel No: 0844 826 1902
Fax: 01603 613886
Training Ground: Colney Training Centre, Hethersett Lane, Colney, Norwich NR4 7TS
Brief History: Founded 1902. Former grounds: Newmarket Road and the Nest, Rosary Road; moved to Carrow Road in 1935. Founder-members 3rd Division (1920). Record attendance 43,984
(Total) Current Capacity: 27,000
Visiting Supporters' Allocation: 2,500 maximum in South Stand
Nearest Railway Station: Norwich
Parking (Car): City centre car parks
Parking (Coach/Bus): Lower Clarence Road
Police Force and Tel No: Norfolk (0845 345 3458)
Disabled Visitors' Facilities:
Wheelchairs: New facility in corner infill stand
Blind: Commentary available
Anticipated Development(s): The £3 million corner infill between the new Jarrold (South) Stand and the River End was opened in two stages in early 2005. The upper tier provides seats for 850 and the lower for 660. There is also a new disabled area located between the two tiers. This work took Carrow Road's capacity to 26,000. As part of the plans for the Jarrold Stand, the pitch was relocated one metre away from the City Stand; this will facilitate the construction of a second tier on the City Stand in the future if required. After a gap of 27 years – it was removed for repair in 1982 – the clock from the City Stand was restored to the building in July 2009. The club announced in May 2010 that it was intending to increase the capacity of Carrow Road to 27,000 by the addition of c1000 seats within the existing stands. The club has long-terms plans to increase capacity to 35,000 should a Premier League place be regained.

▲ 702878
◄ 702868

C Club Offices
S Club Shop

1 Carrow Road
2 A47 King Street
3 River Wensum
4 Riverside
5 Car Park
6 To Norwich station
7 South (Jarrold) Stand
8 Geoffrey Watling (City) Stand
9 Barclay End Stand
10 River End Stand

↑ *North direction (approx)*

nottingham forest

City Ground, Nottingham, NG2 5FJ

website: **WWW.NOTTINGHAMFOREST.CO.UK**
e:mail: **VIA WEBSITE**
tel no: **0115 982 4444**
colours: **RED SHIRTS, WHITE SHORTS**
nickname: **THE REDS**
season 2010/11: **CHAMPIONSHIP**

Last Season: **3rd** (p**46**; w**22**; d**13**; l**11**; gf**65**; ga**40**)

Another of the dark horses in the Championship, Billy Davies's Nottingham Forest appeared in with a shout of an unlikely automatic promotion place for much of the season aided by a run of 19 League matches unbeaten from late September through to the end of January – and it had to be local rivals Derby County that broke the run. Following the 5-0 victory over QPR, Forest were sitting pretty in second place five points clear of West Brom. Thereafter, the season effectively split in two, with the team barely dropping a point at home but away from the City Ground it was another matter as the final nine away matches realised a mere two points. The fact that Forest finished in third place was largely the result of the club's excellent home form – 18 wins and two draws – whereas the club's away form – with only four wins and 11 draws – was closer to relegation form. Finishing third resulted in a Play-Off semi-final against Blackpool, but defeats home and away resulted in the team from Lancashire going through to Wembley on the back of an aggregate 6-4 victory. Thus Forest will again be in the Championship in 2010/11; provided that the team can perform better on its travels then again there is the reasonable hope of a Play-Off place at the very least, particularly given the parlous nature of two of the teams dropping out of the Premier League.

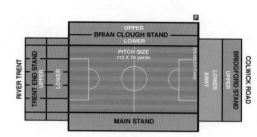

Advance Tickets Tel No: 0871 226 1980
Fax: 0115 982 4455
Training Ground: Nottingham Forest Football Academy, Gresham Close, West Bridgford, Nottingham NG2 7RQ
Brief History: Founded 1865 as Forest Football Club, changed name to Nottingham Forest (c1879). Former Grounds: Forest Recreation Ground, Meadow Cricket Ground, Trent Bridge (Cricket Ground), Parkside, Gregory Ground and Town Ground, moved to City Ground in 1898. Founder-members of Second Division (1892). Record attendance 49,945
(Total) Current Capacity: 30,602 (all seated)
Visiting Supporters' Allocation: Approx 4,750
Nearest Railway Station: Nottingham
Parking (Car): East car park and street parking
Parking (Coach/Bus): East car park
Police Force and Tel No: Nottinghamshire (0300 300 9999)
Disabled Visitors' Facilities:
Wheelchairs: Front of Brian Clough Stand
Blind: No special facility
Anticipated Development(s): In late June 2007 it was announced that the club was planning a possible relocation from the City Ground to a new ground. If all goes according to plan, the club anticipates moving into the new £45-50 million ground for the start of the 2014/15 season. The proposed 45,000-seat new ground was selected as one of the 12 possible grounds for use in 2018 should England win the World Cup. However, Nottinghamshire County Council, owner of the site of the proposed new ground at Gamston, criticised plans in early September 2009 stating that it would not sell the land nor support the development of the ground on a greenfield site.

C Club Offices
S Club Shop
E Entrance(s) for visiting
   supporters

1 Radcliffe Road
2 Lady Bay Bridge Road
3 Trent Bridge
4 Trent Bridge Cricket Ground
5 Bridgford Stand (away)
6 River Trent
7 To Nottingham Midland
   station (½ mile)

↑ North direction (approx)

◄ 703076
▼ 703084

121

notts county

Meadow Lane, Nottingham, NG2 3HJ

website: **WWW.NOTTSCOUNTYFC.CO.UK**
e:mail: **OFFICE@NOTTSCOUNTYFC.CO.UK**
tel no: **0115 952 9000**
colours: **BLACK AND WHITE STRIPED SHIRTS, BLACK SHORTS**
nickname: **THE MAGPIES**
season 2010/11: **LEAGUE ONE**

Last Season: **1st** (promoted) (p**46**; w**27**; d**12**; l**7**; gf**96**; ga**31**)

In years to come there will, no doubt, be books written about the strange goings-on at Meadow Lane during the 2009/10 season The high-profile take-over of County and the subsequent appointment of Sven-Goran Eriksson were always going to lead to dramatic changes at the club and this was to prove the case. With the additional funding available, the club's squad was immeasurably strengthened – although Sol Campbell was only to last a single match – and initially the club seemed destined to run away with the division. However, despite a promising start, County slipped out of the automatic promotion places and, following a 2-2 home draw against Torquay United (a result that left the Magpies in fifth position), Ian McParland departed in mid-October. The club moved quickly to appoint Eriksson's long-term assistant, Hans Backe, to the managerial vacancy. However, in mid-December, after just seven weeks as manager, Backe quit the club. He was replaced as caretaker boss by Dave Kevan before the appointment of the experienced Steve Cotterill. Under Cotterill, the club secured promotion to League One but affairs off the field continued to make greater headlines, with the club again changing hands and Eriksson also departing. Come the end of the season, Cotterill announced that he was not staying as manager and a number of high-profile players, including Kasper Schmeichel, also departed. The new manager, Craig Short, faces a daunting challenge in keeping County in League One given the loss of influential players and the increasing uncertainty about the club's financial viability.

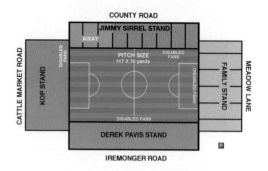

Advance Tickets Tel No: 0115 955 7204
Fax: 0115 955 3994
Training Ground: Highfields, University Boulevard, Nottingham NG7 2PS
Brief History: Founded 1862 (oldest club in Football League) as Nottingham, changed to Notts County in c1882. Former Grounds: Notts Cricket Ground (Beeston), Castle Cricket Ground, Trent Bridge Cricket Ground, moved to Meadow Lane in 1910. Founder-members Football League (1888). Record attendance 47,310
(Total) Current Capacity: 20,300 (all seated)
Visiting Supporters' Allocation: 1,300 in Jimmy Sirrel Stand
Nearest Railway Station: Nottingham Midland
Parking (Car): Mainly street parking
Parking (Coach/Bus): Cattle market
Other clubs sharing ground: Nottingham RUFC
Police Force and Tel No: Nottingham (0300 300 9999)
Disabled Visitors' Facilities:
Wheelchairs: Meadow Lane/Jimmy Sirrel/Derek Pavis Stands
Blind: No special facility

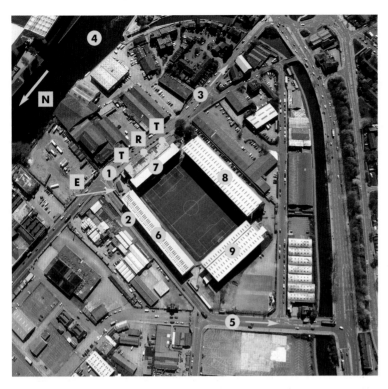

E Entrance(s) for visiting
supporters
R Refreshment bars for visiting
supporters
T Toilets for visiting supporters

1 A6011 Meadow Lane
2 County Road
3 A60 London Road
4 River Trent
5 Nottingham Midland station
(¹/₂ mile)
6 Jimmy Sirrel Stand
7 Family (Meadow Lane) Stand
8 Derek Pavis Stand
9 Kop Stand

↑ North direction (approx)

◄ 703064
▼ 703069

oldham athletic

Boundary Park, Oldham, OL1 2PA

website: **WWW.OLDHAMATHLETIC.CO.UK**
e:mail: **ENQUIRIES@OLDHAMATHLETIC.CO.UK**
tel no: **0161 624 4972**
colours: **BLUE SHIRTS, BLUE SHORTS**
nickname: **THE LATICS**
season 2010/11: **LEAGUE ONE**

Last Season: **16th** (p**46**; w**13**; d**13**; l**20**; gf**39**; ga**57**)

Although highly experienced at this level, Dave Penney's career at Boundary Park was to last just over a year, as he was dismissed in early May following the 3-0 defeat away at Yeovil Town. Although results to the end of October suggested that the club was within a shout of the Play-Offs, inconsistent form thereafter saw the team drift out of contention and finishing in 16th place was ultimately a considerable disappointment. Following the dismissal of Penney, Martin Gray took over as caretaker boss for the final match of the season, a 2-0 home defeat by Charlton Athletic. The new manager, Paul Dickov, will face the challenge of reviving the club's fortunes in an era of tightened budgets but a top-half finish should certainly be a realistic hope for the new season.

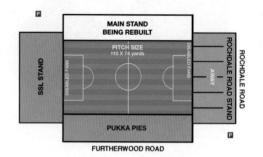

Advance Tickets Tel No: 0610 785 5150
Fax: 0161 627 5915
Training Ground: Chapel Road, Hollins, Oldham OL8 4QQ
Brief History: Founded 1897 as Pine Villa, changed name to Oldham Athletic in 1899. Former Grounds: Berry's Field, Pine Mill, Athletic Ground (later named Boundary Park), Hudson Fold, moved to Boundary Park in 1906. Record attendance 47,671
(Total) Current Capacity: 10,900 (all seated)
Visiting Supporters' Allocation: 1,600 minimum, 4,600 maximum in Rochdale Road Stand
Nearest Railway Station: Oldham Werneth
Parking (Car): Lookers Stand car park
Parking (Coach/Bus): At Ground
Other Clubs Sharing Ground:
Oldham Roughyeads RLFC
Police Force and Tel No: Greater Manchester (0161 872 5050)
Disabled Visitors' Facilities:
Wheelchairs: Rochdale Road and Seton Stands
Blind: No special facility
Anticipated Development(s): Although work started in the summer of 2008 on the reconstruction of Boundary Park with the demolition of the Lookers Stand, the club decided subsequently to relocate to a new site at Failsworth where a new 12,000-seat ground, costing £20 million, is planned. If all goes according to plan the new ground will be completed for the start of the 2011/12 season.

C Club Offices
E Entrance(s) for visiting
  supporters

1 Sheepfoot Lane
2 Furtherwood Road
3 Chadderton Way
4 Westhulme Way
5 To Oldham Werneth station
  (1½ miles) (temporarily
  closed for conversion to
  Metrolink)
6 Car Park
7 Rochdale Road Stand (away)
8 SSL Stand
9 Lookers Stand
  (under redevelopment)
10 Pukka Pies Stand

↑ North direction (approx)

◄ 703244
▼ 703238

Oxford United

Kassam Stadium, Grenoble Road, Blackbird Leys, Oxford OX4 4XP

website: **WWW.OUFC.CO.UK**
e:mail: **ADMIN@OUFC.CO.UK**
tel no: **01865 337500**
colours: **YELLOW SHIRTS, BLACK SHORTS**
nickname: **THE U'S**
season 2010/11: **LEAGUE TWO**

Last Season: **3rd** (promoted) (p**44**; w**25**; d**11**; l**8**; gf**64**; ga**31**)

Under Chris Wilder in his first full season at the Kassam Stadium, it looked as though Oxford United were going to romp home with the Blue Square Premier League title as, for much of the season, the club was top of the table with a considerable points advantage over the chasing pack. However, a run of four draws and a defeat in March allowed chasing Stevenage Borough to overtake the team and, thereafter, it was a battle between the two for the top shot with the Hertfordshire team ultimately proving successful. Finishing eventually in third place, United faced Rushden & Diamonds in the Play-Offs, winning 3-1 on aggregate to set up a final against York City. Victory 3-1 at Wembley sees United return to the Football League after an absence of four years. Like all promoted teams, the club's first challenge will be consolidation at the higher level but United ought to be able to secure a mid-table position with a view to progressing in the future.

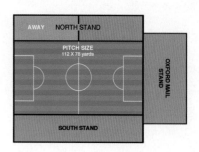

Advance Tickets Tel No: 01865 337533
Fax: 01865 337555
Training Ground: Bicester Sports Association, Chesterton, OX26 1TH
Brief History: Founded in 1893 as Headington (later Headington United), changed name to Oxford United in 1960. Former grounds: Britannia Inn Field, Manor Ground, the Paddocks and the Manor Ground again (from 1925); Moved to new Kassam Stadium in 2001. Elected to the Football League in 1962; relegated to the Conference at the end of the 2005/06 season and promoted back (via the Play-Offs) at the end of the 2009/10 season. Record attendance (at the Manor Ground) 22,730; (at the Kassam Stadium) 12,243
(Total) Current Capacity: 12,500
Visiting Supporters' Allocation: c5,000 (maximum) in North Stand
Nearest Railway Station: Oxford (five miles)
Parking (Car): 1,100 spaces at ground
Parking (Coach/Bus): As directed
Police Force and Tel No: Thames Valley (0845 850 5505)
Disabled Visitors' Facilities:
Wheelchairs: c80 disabled spaces
Blind: No special facility
Anticipated Development(s): Although the club has plans for the construction of the fourth side of the ground there is no confirmed timescale as to when this work will be undertaken.

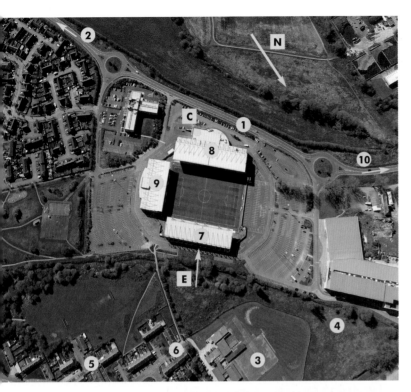

C Club Offices
E Entrance(s) for visiting
   supporters

1 Grenoble Road
2 To A4074
3 Northfield School
4 To Oxford city centre and
   railway station (four/five miles
   respectively)
5 Blackbird Leys Estate
6 Knights Road
7 North Stand (away)
8 South Stand
9 East Stand
10 To B480

↑ *North direction (approx)*

◄ 703040
▼ 703050

peterborough united

London Road, Peterborough, Cambs, PE2 8AL

website: **WWW.THEPOSH.COM**
e:mail: **INFO@THEPOSH.COM**
tel no: **01733 563947**
colours: **BLUE SHIRTS, WHITE SHORTS**
nickname: **POSH**
season 2010/11: **LEAGUE ONE**

Last Season: **24th** (relegated) (p**46**; w**8**; d**10**; l**28**; gf**28**; ga**80**)

After two promotions in two seasons, life in the Championship was always going to prove a struggle for Posh and, after a poor start to the campaign, Darren Ferguson left London Road with the club quickly acting to bring Mark Cooper in as his replacement. The new regime was, however, to be short-lived as, following 13 matches in charge which brought only one victory, Cooper was sacked in early February following a 2-0 defeat at Crystal Palace, a result that left Posh 11 points from safety in last spot. The club again acted quickly, bringing in Jim Gannon who had had considerable success previously at Stockport. Towards the end of the season it was announced that Gannon was not to stay beyond the end of the campaign and he stood down in early April, following the 2-2 draw at Barnsley that confirmed Posh's relegation back to League One. The following day it was announced that ex-Bristol City boss Gary Johnson would replace Gannon for the remainder of the season and take charge for 2010/11. As a relegated team, Posh ought to be one of those featuring in the promotion battle but a Play-Off place is perhaps the best that the London Road faithful can look forward to.

Advance Tickets Tel No: 0844 847 1934
Fax: 01733 344140
Training Ground: Woodlands, Slash Lane, Castor, Peterborough PE5 7BD
Brief History: Founded in 1934 (no connection with former 'Peterborough and Fletton United' FC). Elected to Football League in 1960. Record attendance 30,096
(Total) Current Capacity: 15,314 (7,669 seated)
Visiting Supporters' Allocation: 4,758 (756 seated)
Nearest Railway Station: Peterborough
Parking (Car): Peterborough
Parking (Coach/Bus): At ground
Police Force and Tel No: Cambridgeshire (0345 456 4564)
Disabled Visitors' Facilities:
Wheelchairs: South Stand
Blind: No special facility
Future Development(s): The club announced in mid-January 2007 that it was examining the possibility of seeking planning permission to replace the existing terraced Moys End Stand with a new 2,000-seat stand as part of a five-year plan that could ultimately see London Road converted into an all-seater stadium.

C Club Offices
S Club Shop
E Entrance(s) for visiting supporters
R Refreshment bars for visiting supporters
T Toilets for visiting supporters

1 A15 London Road
2 Car Parks
3 Peterborough station (1 mile)
4 Glebe Road
5 A605
6 To A1 (north) (5 miles)
7 Main Stand
8 To Whittlesey
9 To A1 (south) (5 miles)
10 Norwich & Peterborough Stand
11 London Road Terrace
12 Moys Terrace (away)

↑ North direction (approx)

◄ 702880
▼ 702889

plymouth argyle

Home Park, Plymouth, PL2 3DQ

website: **WWW.PAFC.CO.UK**
e:mail: **ARGYLE@PAFC.CO.UK**
tel no: **01752 562561**
colours: **WHITE AND GREEN SHIRTS, WHITE SHORTS**
nickname: **THE PILGRIMS**
season 2010/11: **LEAGUE ONE**

Last Season: **23rd** (relegated) (p**46**; w**11**; d**8**; l**27**; gf**43**; ga**68**)

With Argyle struggling towards the bottom end of the Championship table, the club decided to relieve Paul Sturrock, manager since November 2007, of his control of the team in early December 2009 although he was to remain at the club in a business support role. In his place ex-Plymouth striker Paul Mariner, who had rejoined the club earlier in the season as head coach, was appointed to take charge of the squad. Mariner's first game in charge resulted in a 2-0 defeat away at Preston North End and, with the team winning only five of its last 25 matches, results led to the team's relegation back to League One after six seasons in the Championship. During the course of the 2009/10 season, Mariner's hands were tied briefly by an embargo on transfers; this was lifted in January but constrained Mariner's activities during that month's transfer window. As a relegated team, Argyle ought, potentially, to be one of the favourite clubs to make an impact in the chase for the Play-Offs at least. However, much will depend on the new players that new boss, the hugely experienced Peter Reid, is able to bring to the club given that it was announced at the end of the season that Mariner would not be at the helm for the new season.

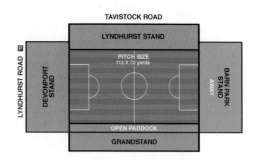

Advance Tickets Tel No: 0845 338 7232
Fax: 01752 606167
Training Ground: Adjacent to ground
Brief History: Founded 1886 as Argyle Athletic Club, changed name to Plymouth Argyle in 1903. Founder-members Third Division (1920). Record attendance 43,596
(Total) Current Capacity: 19,500 (all seated)
Visiting Supporters' Allocation: 1,300 (all seated) in Barn Park End Stand up to maximum of 2,000
Nearest Railway Station: Plymouth
Parking (Car): Car park adjacent
Parking (Coach/Bus): Central car park
Police Force and Tel No: Devon & Cornwall (08452 777444)
Disabled Visitors' Facilities:
Wheelchairs: Devonport End
Blind: Commentary available
Anticipated Development(s): The club had hoped to have plans in place by the end of 2009 for the construction of a new Main Stand. The construction of the new stand would see Home Park's capacity increase to 25,000. The ground was also selected as one of the 12 possible grounds for use in 2018 should England win the World Cup. If the bid proves successful, the ground's capacity would need to be raised to 44,000.

C Club Offices
S Club Shop

1 A386 Outland Road
2 Car Park
3 Devonport Road
4 Central Park
5 Town Centre & Plymouth
   station (½ mile)
6 To A38 (½ mile)
7 Grandstand
8 Lyndhurst Stand
9 Devonport End
10 Barn Park End (away)

↑ North direction (approx)

◄ 702815
▼ 702812

portsmouth

Fratton Park, Frogmore Road, Southsea, Portsmouth, PO4 8RA

website: **WWW.PORTSMOUTHFC.CO.UK**
e:mail: **INFO@POMPEYFC.CO.UK**
tel no: **02392 731204**
colours: **BLUE SHIRTS, WHITE SHORTS**
nickname: **POMPEY**
season 2010/11: **CHAMPIONSHIP**

Last Season: **20th*** (relegated) (p**38**; w**7**; d**7**; l**24**; gf**34**; ga**66**)

A hugely difficult season for Pompey both on and off the field saw the club enter Administration – the first club in the Premier League to suffer this fate – in February and thus receive an automatic nine-point deduction. The club was already struggling on the field and this deduction effectively ensured the team's relegation. Earlier in the season, the club's poor start to the campaign on the field had resulted in the dismissal in November of Paul Hart as manager after only nine months in the job and his replacement by ex-Chelsea boss Avram Grant. In an otherwise dire season, there was one great success: the club's FA Cup run. Despite the financial problems, which saw players depart and other players help to pay the wages of some of the backroom staff, the club battled through to the final defeating Tottenham 2-0 in the semi-final. Ironically, it was the club's appearance and victory in the FA Cup final in 2008 that sparked many of the financial commitments that led the club to ruin. With uncertainty over which players would be available for the final stages of the cup run, the final itself was a case of so near yet so far. Although Chelsea dominated and proved victorious by a single goal, it could have been so different had Boateng's penalty attempt not been saved. With the romance of the cup out of the way, the fact is that Pompey are now in the Championship and in a weak position financially. Avram Grant, as expected, has departed as manager and his replacement, Steve Cotterill, will face a severe challenge in putting together a squad capable of maintaining even a place in the Championship. The harsh reality is that the club will have a severe battle to retain its Championship status come May 2011.

Advance Tickets Tel No: 0844 847 1898
Fax: 02392 734129
Club Office: Rodney Road, Portsmouth, PO4 8SX
Training Ground: Stoneham Lane, Eastleigh SO50 9HT
Brief History: Founded 1898. Founder-members Third Division (1920). Record attendance 51,385
(Total) Current Capacity: 20,700 (all seated)
Visiting Supporters' Allocation: 2,000 (max) in Milton Stand
Nearest Railway Station: Fratton
Parking (Car): Street parking
Parking (Coach/Bus): As directed by Police
Police Force and Tel No: Hampshire (02392 321111)
Disabled Visitors' Facilities:
Wheelchairs: Fratton End Stand
Blind: No special facility

Anticipated Development(s): The club's original plans for relocation to a site close to the city's naval dockyard brought objections from the Royal Navy and, as a result, the club identified a new site for the construction of a 36,000-seat ground at Horsea Island. Planning permission for the new ground was to be sought in 2008 with an original anticipated completion date of the start of the 2011/12 season. As a temporary measure a roof was installed over the Milton End during the 2007/08 season. However, the credit crunch has caused a rethink and, in early 2009, it was announced that in the short term the club would redevelop Fratton Park into a 30,000-seat ground. This work will entail rotating the pitch 90 degrees, the construction of two new stands, the enlargement of the Fratton End and improvement of the existing South Stand. If planning permission is gained, then work would have started quickly. Work on Fratton Park has yet to start and in the current circumstances nothing would appear to be confirmed. The relocation scheme will, however, continue to be developed with a view to completion in 2018 and possible use should England gain the World Cup that year.

* Nine-point deduction for entering Administration during the course of the season.

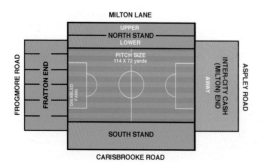

C Club Offices
S Club Shop
E Entrance(s) for visiting supporters
R Refreshment bars for visiting supporters
T Toilets for visiting supporters

1 Alverstone Road
2 Carisbrook Road
3 A288 Milton Road
4 A2030 Velder Avenue A27
5 A2030 Goldsmith Avenue
6 Fratton station (½ mile)
7 Fratton End
8 Milton End
9 North Stand
10 South Stand

↑ *North direction (approx)*

◄ 701219
▼ 701226

port vale

Vale Park, Burslem, Stoke-on-Trent, ST6 1AW

website: **WWW.PORT-VALE.CO.UK**
e:mail: **ENQUIRIES@PORT-VALE.CO.UK**
tel no: **01782 655800**
colours: **WHITE/BLACK SHIRTS, BLACK SHORTS**
nickname: **THE VALIANTS**
season 2010/11: **LEAGUE TWO**

Last Season: **10th** (p**46**; w**17**; d**17**; l**12**; gf**61**; ga**50**)

Ultimately a slightly disappointing season for the Valiants as Micky Adams' team struggled to make an impact in League Two, hovering in mid-table for much of the campaign. The early part of the season – with Carling Cup victories at Sheffield United in the 1st round and at home to Sheffield Wednesday in the 2nd – suggested that the team might have the potential to make a push towards the Play-Offs, but inconsistent League form put paid to any realistic chance of making the top seven. Form over the latter part of the season, with nine wins and four draws in the club's final 18 League matches, does, however, offer some hope that, suitably strengthened, the team should prosper in 2010/11 with the Play-Offs being a realistic expectation.

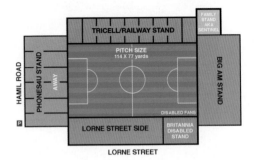

Advance Tickets Tel No: 01782 655832
Fax: 01782 834981
Training Ground: Adjacent to ground
Brief History: Founded 1876 as Burslem Port Vale, changed name to 'Port Vale' in 1907 (reformed club). Former Grounds: The Meadows Longport, Moorland Road Athletic Ground, Cobridge Athletic Grounds, Recreation Ground Hanley, moved to Vale Park in 1950. Founder-members Second Division (1892). Record attendance 49,768
(Total) Current Capacity: 18,947 (all seated)
Visiting Supporters' Allocation: 4,550
(in Hamil Road [Phones4U] Stand)
Nearest Railway Station: Longport (two miles)
Parking (Car): Car park at Ground
Parking (Coach/Bus): Hamil Road car park
Police Force and Tel No: Staffordshire (0300 123 4455)
Disabled Visitors' Facilities:
Wheelchairs: 20 spaces in new Britannic Disabled Stand
Blind: Commentary availaable
Anticipated Development(s): After some years with the stand half finished, the club's new owners completed the roof over the Lorne Street Stand during the 2004/05 season. The Club had planned to install seats in the remainder of the stand during the 2007/08 season but this is still to be undertaken.

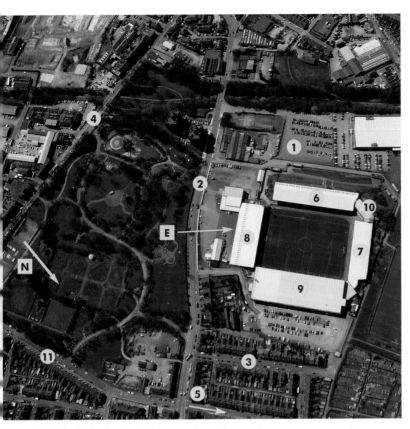

E Entrance(s) for visiting
   supporters

 1 Car Parks
 2 Hamil Road
 3 Lorne Street
 4 B5051 Moorland Road
 5 To Burslem Town Centre
 6 Railway Stand
 7 Big Am Stand
 8 Hamil Road Stand
 9 Lorne Street Stand
10 Family Section
11 Park Road

↑ North direction (approx)

◄ 703052
▼ 703054

preston north end

Deepdale, Sir Tom Finney Way, Preston, PR1 6RU

website: **WWW.PNEFC.NET**
e:mail: **ENQUIRIES@PNE.COM**
tel no: **0844 856 1964**
colours: **WHITE SHIRTS, BLUE SHORTS**
nickname: **THE LILYWHITES**
season 2010/11: **CHAMPIONSHIP**

Last Season: **17th** (p**46**; w**13**; d**15**; l**18**; gf**58**; ga**73**)

Although Preston made a reasonable start to the 2009/10 season, averaging two points a game for the first nine matches, a dip in form that saw the team gain only two wins in the next 14 matches saw the club drop to 16th in the Championship and saw Alan Irvine depart the managerial hot-seat at the end of December. Following Irvine's departure, the club appointed Darren Ferguson, who'd left Peterborough United in November, to the position of manager in early January. The second half of the season was, if anything, worse than the first as the team gained only 25 points in the last 23 League games, having gathered 29 from the first 23, and thus finished in a disappointing 17th place. With the season over, Ferguson will aim to rebuild the team with the hope of mounting a significant challenge for the Play-Offs again. With two relatively weak teams being relegated from the Premier League in 2009/10 in financially-challenged Hull City and Portsmouth, the opportunity is there for some of the more ambitious Championship teams to capitalise and, having reached the Play-Offs at the end of 2008/09, Preston has the pedigree to do so again in 2010/11.

Advance Tickets Tel No: 0844 856 1966
Fax: 01772 693366
Training Ground: Springfields Sports Ground, Dodney Drive, Lea, Preston PR2 1XR
Brief History: Founded 1867 as a Rugby Club, changed to soccer in 1881. Former ground: Moor Park, moved to (later named) Deepdale in 1875. Founder-members Football League (1888). Record attendance 42,684
(Total) Current Capacity: 23,403 (all seated)
Visiting Supporters' Allocation: 6,000 maximum in Bill Shankly Stand
Nearest Railway Station: Preston (2 miles)
Parking (Car): West Stand car park
Parking (Coach/Bus): West Stand car park
Police Force and Tel No: Lancashire (0845 125 3545)
Disabled Visitors' Facilities:
Wheelchairs: Tom Finney Stand and Bill Shankly Stand
Blind: Earphones Commentary

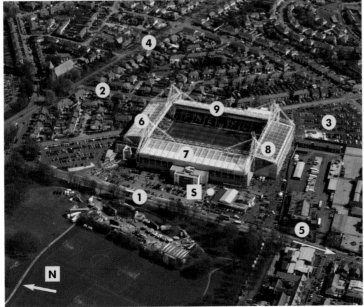

▲ 702161
◀ 702169

5 Club Shop

1 A6033 Deepdale Road
2 Lowthorpe Road
3 Car Park
4 A5085 Blackpool Road
5 Preston station
　(2 miles)
6 Bill Shankly Stand
7 Tom Finney Stand
8 Town End Stand
9 Invincibles Pavilion stand

↑ *North direction (approx)*

queens park rangers

Loftus Road Stadium, South Africa Road, London, W12 7PA

website: **WWW.QPR.CO.UK**
e:mail: **BOXOFFICE@QPR.CO.UK**
tel no: **020 8743 0262**
colours: **BLUE AND WHITE HOOPED SHIRTS, WHITE SHORTS**
nickname: **THE SUPERHOOPS**
season 2010/11: **CHAMPIONSHIP**

Last Season: **13th** (p**46**; w**14**; d**15**; l**17**; gf**58**; ga**65**)

In early December manager Jim Magilton was suspended by the club following the 3-1 defeat at Watford when an alleged incident took place between the manager and one of the team. Although Magilton strenuously denied any wrongdoing, it was announced in mid-December that he had left the club. Paul Hart, appointed manager two days later, was destined to have one of the shortest managerial reigns of recent years, lasting only five games at Loftus Road before being dismissed in mid-January after the 3-2 home defeat by Sheffield United in the FA Cup. He was succeeded as caretaker-manager by Mick Harford although the rumours linking Crystal Palace boss Neil Warnock to the job proved well-founded when he was appointed in early March. Warnock inherited a team in 20th place, only three points above the drop zone. However, his arrival saw an almost immediate return to form – with two victories (including a 2-0 triumph over promotion-chasing West Brom) – in his first two matches and only four defeats in the club's last 14 League matches. With high profile and wealthy backers, QPR are an undoubtedly ambitious team and in Neil Warnock the club has a manager highly experienced in Championship football. As a result, Rangers ought to be one of the teams vying for the Play-Offs at the very least in 2010/11.

Advance Tickets Tel No: 0844 477 7007
Fax: 020 8749 0994
Training Ground: Imperial College Sports Ground, Sipson Lane, Harlington, Middlesex UB3 5AQ
Brief History: Founded 1885 as 'St. Jude's Institute', amalgamated with Christchurch Rangers to become Queens Park Rangers in 1886. Football League record number of former Grounds and Ground moves (13 different venues, 17 changes), including White City Stadium (twice); final move to Loftus Road in 1963. Founder-members Third Division (1920). Record attendance (at Loftus Road) 35,353.
(Total) Current Capacity: 19,130 (all seated)
Visiting Supporters' Allocation: 2,500 (maximum) in School End
Nearest Railway Station: Shepherds Bush and White City (both tube)
Parking (Car): White City NCP and street parking
Parking (Coach/Bus): White City NCP
Police Force and Tel No: Metropolitan (0300 123 1212)
Disabled Visitors' Facilities:
Wheelchairs: Ellerslie Road Stand and West Paddock
Blind: Ellerslie Road Stand
Anticipated Development(s): There is vague talk of possible relocation, but nothing has been confirmed. Given the constrained site occupied by Loftus Road, it will be difficult to increase the existing ground's capacity.

C Club Offices
S Club Shop
E Entrance(s) for visiting
   supporters

1 South Africa Road
2 To White City tube station,
   A219 Wood Lane and A40
   Western Avenue
3 A4020 Uxbridge Road
4 To Shepherds Bush tube
   station
5 Ellerslie Road Stand
6 BBC Television Centre
7 Loftus Road
8 Bloemfontein Road

↑ North direction (approx)

◀ 700895
▼ 700889

reading

Madejski Stadium, Bennet Road, Reading, RG2 0FL

website: **WWW.READINGFC.CO.UK**
e:mail: **CUSTOMERSERVICE@READINGFC.CO.UK**
tel no: **0118 968 1100**
colours: **WHITE WITH BLUE HOOPS SHIRTS, BLUE SHORTS**
nickname: **THE ROYALS**
season 2010/11: **CHAMPIONSHIP**

Last Season: **9th (p46; w17; d12; l17; gf86; ga63)**

Although he was only appointed in the summer, Brendan Rodgers's reign at Reading proved to be relatively short, lasting only six months until he left the club by mutual consent in mid-December 2009. He departed from the club after a 1-1 draw at home against fellow strugglers Scunthorpe United, a result that left Reading in 21st place only three points above the drop zone. During Rodgers's tenure the team achieved only one home victory in the League, 2-1 against Blackpool. He was replaced, initially as caretaker but confirmed in the post in late January following the team's excellent FA Cup results against Liverpool (winning 2-1 after extra time at Anfield in a replay in the 3rd Round) and Burnley at home 1-0 in the 4th, by Brian McDermott. Under McDermott, the club's impressive run in the FA Cup continued with victory away at West Brom in the 5th round replay before succumbing 4-2 to Aston Villa. Away from the League, McDermott inherited a club in 21st position in the Championship and under his stewardship form improved and the season ended with the team in ninth place, only seven points off the Play-Offs – much better than it looked at one stage. However, not all in the garden is rosy; having been in the Championship now for two seasons, the Premier League parachute payments will cease for the 2010/11 campaign and the club will face a battle with other ex-Premier League teams for promotion. Realistically, a top-half finish should be achievable with the Play-Offs an outside bet.

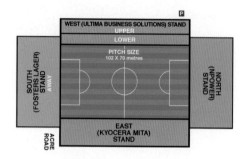

Advance Tickets Tel No: 0844 249 1871
Fax: 0118 968 1101

Training Ground: Reading FC Academy Training Ground, Hogwood Lane, Arborfield Garrison, Wokingham RG40 4QW

Brief History: Founded 1871. Amalgamated with Reading Hornets in 1877 and with Earley in 1889. Former Grounds: Reading Recreation Ground, Reading Cricket Ground, Coley Park, Caversham Cricket Ground and Elm Park (1895-1998); moved to the Madejski Stadium at the start of the 1998/99 season. Founder-members of the Third Division in 1920. Record attendance (at Elm Park) 33,042; (at Madejski Stadium) 24,122

(Total) Current Capacity: 24,200 (all seated)

Visiting Supporters' Allocation: 4,300 (maximum in the Fosters Lager South Stand)

Nearest Railway Station: Reading (2.5 miles)

Parking (Car): 1,800-space car park at the ground, 700 of these spaces are reserved

Parking (Coach/Bus): As directed

Other Clubs Sharing Ground: London Irish RUFC

Police Force and Tel No: Thames Valley (0845 850 5505)

Disabled Visitors' Facilities:

Wheelchairs: 128 designated spaces on all four sides of the ground

Blind: 12 places for match day commentaries

Anticipated Development(s): The club applied for Planning Permission to expand the capacity of the Madejski Stadium by 14,000 seats in October 2005, taking the ground's capacity up from 24,000 to 38,000. Permission was subsequently granted and will involve extending the North, South and East stands. Work was scheduled to start in the summer of 2008 with an anticipated completion date of the end of 2009. Work has, however, yet to start on the ground's extension. A new station – Reading Green Park – on the line from Reading to Basingstoke is scheduled to open in 2010 to serve the Green Park Business Park and the Madejski Stadium.

C Club Offices
S Club Shop

1 North Stand
2 East Stand
3 South Stand (away)
4 West Stand
5 A33 Basingstoke Road
6 A33 to M4 (Jct 11)
7 A33 to Reading Town Centre
and station (two miles)
8 Hurst Way
9 Boot End

⬆ *North direction (approx)*

◄ 702329
▼ 702341

rochdale

Spotland Stadium, Willbutts Lane, Rochdale, OL11 5DS

website: **WWW.ROCHDALEAFC.CO.UK**
e:mail: **OFFICE@ROCHDALEAFC.CO.UK**
tel no: **0844 826 1907**
colours: **BLUE SHIRTS, BLUE SHORTS**
nickname: **THE DALE**
season 2010/11: **LEAGUE ONE**

Last Season: **3rd** (promoted) (p**46**; w**25**; d**7**; l**14**; gf**82**; ga**48**)

Having just missed out on promotion yet again through the Play-Offs at the end of the 2008/09 season, Rochdale's unenviable record as the longest-standing member of League Two finally came to an end with promotion achieved back to League One. Under Keith Hill the Dale had been in the hunt for automatic promotion throughout the season although a late dip in form had allowed the chasing teams to believe that, once again, the team had bottled promotion at the end. Following a run of three defeats and a draw, automatic promotion was achieved in mid-April with the 1-0 victory over Play-Off-chasing Northampton Town at Spotland. With promotion confirmed, the scene became one of a serious party. The club's last promotion from the League's basement division was at the end of the 1968/69 season; on that occasions the club managed to survive five years in the old Third Division before relegation back to the fourth. As with all promoted teams, Keith Hill's initial aspiration will be to secure League One status come May 2011 and probably anything above 20th place will be considered a success.

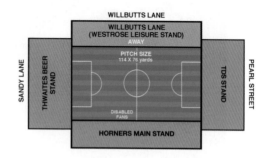

Advance Tickets Tel No: 0844 826 1907

Fax: 01706 648466

Training Ground: No specific facility

Brief History: Founded 1907 from former Rochdale Town F.C. (founded 1900). Founder-members Third Division North (1921). Record attendance 24,231

(Total) Current Capacity: 10,262; (8,342 seated)

Visiting Supporters' Allocation: 3,650 maximum (seated) in Willbutts Lane (Westrose Leisure) Stand

Nearest Railway Station: Rochdale

Parking (Car): Rear of ground

Parking (Coach/Bus): Rear of ground

Other Clubs Sharing Ground: Rochdale Hornets RLFC

Police Force and Tel No: Greater Manchester (0161 872 5050)

Disabled Visitors' Facilities:

Wheelchairs: Main, WMG and Willbutts Lane stands – disabled area

Blind: Commentary available

Anticipated Development(s): None following completion of Willbutts Lane Stand.

C Club Offices
S Club Shop
E Entrance(s) for visiting
   supporters

1 Willbutts Lane
2 A627 Edenfield Road
3 Rochdale station
   (½ mile)
4 Sandy Lane
5 To M62
6 To M65 and North
7 Pearl Street Stand
8 Willbutts Lane (Westrose
   Leisure) Stand (away)
9 Thwaites Beer Stand
10 Main Stand

↑ North direction (approx)

◄ 701829
▼ 701848

rotherham united

Don Valley Stadium, Worksop Road, Sheffield, S9 3TL

website: **WWW.THEMILLERS.CO.UK**
e:mail: **OFFICE@ROTHERHAMUNITED.NET**
tel no: **0844 414 0733**
colours: **RED SHIRTS, WHITE SHORTS**
nickname: **THE MILLERS**
season 2010/11: **LEAGUE TWO**

Last Season: **5th** (p46; w21; d10; l15; gf55; ga52)

Although the Millermen were riding high in League Two at the start of September, the club agreed to release Mark Robins to take over as boss of managerless neighbours Barnsley following a compensation deal. Later in month it was announced that Ronnie Moore, who'd managed the team between 1997 and 2005 and who'd taken the team to Division One in 2001, was to return as boss. For much of the campaign it looked as though the team would fill one of the three automatic promotion places but a run of five defeats and two draws in the club's last nine League fixtures saw the club miss out on automatic promotion but secure a place in Play-Offs. With victories home and away against Aldershot, winning 3-0 on aggregate, Rotherham faced Dagenham & Redbridge in the final at Wembley. In a pulsating match, the London side was ultimately to emerge as 3-2 victors thus ensuring that Rotherham remain in League Two for another season. Away from the League, Rotherham suffered the embarrassment of being defeated 3-0 away by non-League Luton Town in the FA Cup 2nd round replay but did claim the notable scalp of Derby County in the 1st round of the Carling Cup, winning 2-1 at the Don Valley Stadium. With Moore in charge, Rotherham will again be fancied to make the Play-Offs at least in 2010/11 with automatic promotion a real possibility.

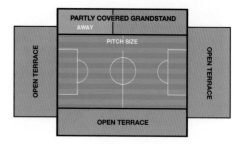

Advance Tickets Tel No: 0844 414 0737
Fax: 0844 414 0744
Club Offices: Mangham House, Mangham Road, Barbot Hall Industrial Estate, Rotherham S61 4RJ
Training Ground: Hooton Training Ground, Thomas Street, Kilnhurst, Mexborough S64 5TF
Brief History: Founded 1877 (as Thornhill later Thornhill United), changed named to Rotherham County in 1905 and to Rotherham United in 1925 (amalgamated with Rotherham Town – Football League members 1893-97 – in 1925). Former Grounds include Red House Ground and Clifton Lane Cricket Ground, moved to Millmoor in 1907 and to the Don Valley Stadium in 2008. Record attendance (at Millmoor): 25,170; (at Don Valley Stadium) 5,404
(Total) Current Capacity: 25,000; however, only the partially-covered Main Stand is used for football with the three open sides unused
Visiting Supporters' Allocation: North End of Main Stand
Nearest Railway Station: Arena / Don Valley Stadium stop on Sheffield Supertram network is 100m from the ground; Sheffield Supertram provides a link between the two nearest main line stations – Sheffield (two miles approx) and Meadowhall (1.5 miles approx)
Parking (Car): As directed
Parking (Coach/Bus): As directed
Other Clubs Sharing Ground: Sheffield Eagles RLFC
Police Force and Tel No: South Yorkshire (0114 220 2020)
Disabled Visitors' Facilities:
Wheelchairs: 12 wheelchair spaces
Blind: No special facility
Anticipated Development(s): In late January it was announced that the club had identified the site of the former Guest & Chrimes foundry as the site of a new £20 million 12,000-seat stadium in the town. If all goes according to plan, the new ground should be completed for the start of the 2012/13 season.

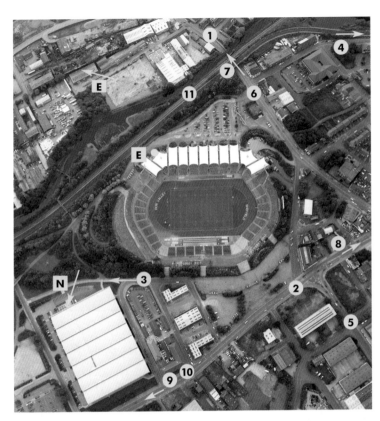

E Entrance(s) for visiting supporters

1 B6085 Darnall Road
2 A6178 Attercliffe Road
3 To Arena/Don Valley Stadium Supertram stop (one mile)
4 To Attercliffe Supertram stop (one mile)
5 B6083 Newhall Road
6 Worksop Road
7 To A6012 and Darnall railway station (two miles)
8 To Sheffield city centre and main line railway station (2½ miles)
9 To M1 Junction 34 (South) (1½ miles)
10 To Rotherham town centre (four miles)
11 Supertram route and freight-only railway line

↑ North direction (approx)

◄ 701360
▼ 701366

scunthorpe united

Glanford Park, Doncaster Road, Scunthorpe, DN15 8TD

website: **WWW.SCUNTHORPE–UNITED.CO.UK**
e:mail: **ADMIN@SCUNTHORPE–UNITED.CO.UK**
tel no: **0871 221 1899**
colours: **CLARET AND BLUE SHIRTS, CLARET SHORTS**
nickname: **THE IRON**
season 2010/11: **CHAMPIONSHIP**

Last Season: **20th** (p**46**; w**14**; d**10**; l**22**; gf**62**; ga**84**)

Promoted at the end of the 2008/09 season, Scunthorpe's season in the Championship was always going to be a battle to avoid repeating the 2007/08 season when again they had achieved promotion but were only to last a single season at this level. Initially Nigel Adkins' team seemed destined for a position of some mid-table safety but a mid-season loss of form, that saw them win one of 10 League matches saw the Iron drift towards the drop zone. Grinding out results thereafter somehow managed to keep the team from being sucked too deep into the relegation mire, although fans were inevitably concerned, and finishing in 20th place, five points above Sheffield Wednesday, can perhaps be regarded as a reasonable success. Away from the League, Scunthorpe must have become heartily sick of Manchester City as the Eastlands' moneybags knocked them out of both the Carling and FA cups. For 2010/11, the challenge will again be to repeat the escape act but, with teams like Norwich being promoted, this could be a much greater problem this time round and the probability is that the club will struggle to survive at this level come May 2011.

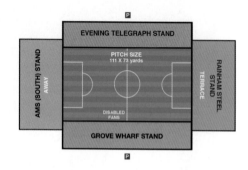

Advance Tickets Tel No: 0871 221 1899
Fax: 01724 857986
Training Ground: Grange Farm, Neap House Road, Gunness, Scunthorpe DN15 8TX
Brief History: Founded 1899 as Scunthorpe United, amalgamated with North Lindsey to become 'Scunthorpe & Lindsey United' in 1912. Changed name to Scunthorpe United in 1956. Former Grounds: Crosby (Lindsey United) and Old Showground, moved to Glanford Park in 1988. Elected to Football League in 1950. Record attendance 8,921 (23,935 at Old Showground)
(Total) Current Capacity: 9,183; (6,400 seated)
Visiting Supporters' Allocation: 1,650 (all seated) in AMS (South) Stand
Nearest Railway Station: Scunthorpe
Parking (Car): At ground
Parking (Coach/Bus): At ground
Police Force and Tel No: Humberside (0845 60 60 222)
Disabled Visitors' Facilities:
Wheelchairs: Grove Wharf Stand
Blind: Commentary available
Anticipated Development(s): The club is seeking planning permission to redevelop the North (Rainham Steel) Stand at Glanford Park with the intention of increasing the ground's capacity to 11,000. In addition, the club is also looking at the possibility of a further relocation, although nothing is confirmed at the present time.

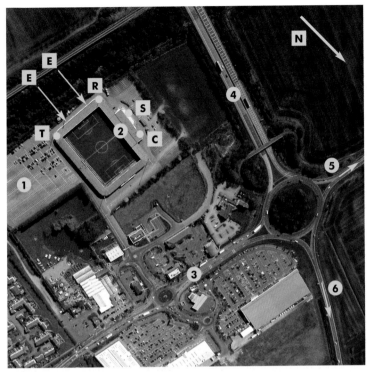

C Club Offices
S Club Shop
E Entrance(s) for visiting
    supporters
R Refreshment bars for visiting
    supporters
T Toilets for visiting supporters

1 Car Park
2 Evening Telegraph Stand
3 A18 to Scunthorpe station
    and Town Centre (1½ miles)
4 M181 and
    M180 Junction 3
5 A18 to Doncaster
6 To Barton on Humber

↑ *North direction (approx)*

◄ 702967
▼ 702977

sheffield united

Bramall Lane, Sheffield, S2 4SU

website: **WWW.SUFC.CO.UK**
e:mail: **INFO@SUFC.CO.UK**
tel no: **0871 995 1899**
colours: **RED AND WHITE STRIPED SHIRTS, BLACK SHORTS**
nickname: **THE BLADES**
season 2010/11: **CHAMPIONSHIP**

Last Season: **8th** (p**46**; w**17**; d**14**; l**15**; gf**62**; ga**55**)

A hugely disappointing season at Bramall Lane saw Sheffield United fail to sustain a serious challenge for either automatic promotion or the Play-Offs. A poor start to the season, which saw the Blades win only four of the first 14 League matches and succumb to an embarrassing 2-1 home defeat in the 1st round of the Carling Cup to League Two Port Vale, set the tempo for mid-table mediocrity. Although the end of season – with three wins and a draw in the final four matches – raised the team to eighth place, fans seem to believe that Kevin Blackwell is not the manager to see the team reclaim a place in the Premier League. Locally, fans will have had the pleasure of seeing rivals Wednesday relegated although this counts as little, one suspects, in the club's ambition to get back to the top flight. As with other ambitious Championship teams, 2010/11 offers a good chance to make a push for the Play-Offs at least given that both Hull City and Portsmouth are financially disadvantaged in coming down from the Premier League and, despite any parachute payments, may struggle at this level. The Blades ought to be vying for the top-six places and failure to do so could lead to change at the top.

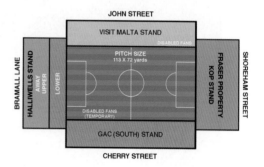

Advance Tickets Tel No: 0871 995 1889

Fax: 0871 663 2430

Training Ground: The Hallam FM Academy @ Sheffield United, 614A Firshill Crescent, Sheffield S4 7DJ

Brief History: Founded 1889. (Sheffield Wednesday occasionally used Bramall Lane c1880.) Founder-members 2nd Division (1892). Record attendance 68,287

(Total) Current Capacity: 32,702 (all seated)

Visiting Supporters' Allocation: 3,000 (seated) can be increased to 5,200 if needed in Halliwells (Bramall Lane) Stand

Nearest Railway Station: Sheffield Midland

Parking (Car): Street parking

Parking (Coach/Bus): As directed by Police

Police Force and Tel No: South Yorkshire (0114 220 2020)

Disabled Visitors' Facilities:

Wheelchairs: South Stand

Blind: Commentary available

Anticipated Development(s): The first phase of the ground's upgrade, taking capacity to 37,000 sees removing the columns from the Kop Stand and other works. More substantial is work proposed for the second phase; this will see the construction of a second tier on the South Stand accommodating 6,000 and ultimately resulting in a new capacity of 44,000. Following the FA's decision to select Hillsborough as a possible World Cup stadium for 2018, the club has announced that work on the expansion of Bramall Lane will be deferred until a place in the Premier League is regained and maintained.

C Club Offices
S Club Shop
E Entrance(s) for visiting
  supporters

1 A621 Bramall Lane
2 Shoreham Street
3 Car Park
4 Sheffield Midland station (¼
  mile)
5 John Street
6 Fraser Property Kop Stand
7 Visit Malta Stand
8 Bramall Lane
  (Halliwells) Stand
9 GAC (South) Stand

↑ North direction (approx)

◄ 702290
▼ 702307

sheffield wednesday

Hillsborough, Sheffield, S6 1SW

website: **WWW.SWFC.CO.UK**
e:mail: **ENQUIRIES@SWFC.CO.UK**
tel no: **0871 995 1867**
colours: **BLUE AND WHITE STRIPED SHIRTS, BLACK SHORTS**
nickname: **THE OWLS**
season 2010/11: **LEAGUE ONE**

Last Season: **22nd** (relegated) (**p46**; w**11**; d**14**; l**21**; gf**49**; ga**69**)

Following a 3-0 defeat at Leicester City, the ninth League game without a victory that resulted in the Owls falling into the drop zone, Brian Laws departed as manager in mid-December. Following further League reversals, the experienced ex-Preston boss, Alan Irvine, was appointed the club's new manager in early January and, under him, there was an immediate improvement in form with the club winning four of his first five matches in charge. However, this improvement was not to last and a sequence of two wins in the club's final 16 League matches meant that, but for Crystal Palace's descent into Administration, the Owls would have been relegated before the end of the campaign. The irony was that the final League game of the season pitched Wednesday at home to the Eagles, with home fans knowing that nothing less than a home win would secure Championship status. With the Owls 2-1 down approaching the final whistle, all looked over but a late equaliser brought renewed hope – particularly when the fourth official indicated a minimum of five minutes added time. Unfortunately for home fans, however, despite coming close, Wednesday failed to score again and so League One football will be on offer at Hillsborough in 2010/11. As a relegated team, Wednesday will be expected to be in the hunt for the Play-Offs at the very least but, as Leeds United and others have discovered, it's not easy to achieve an immediate return.

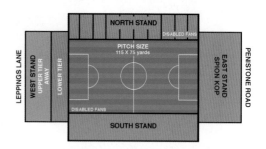

Advance Tickets Tel No: 0871 900 1867
Fax: 0114 221 2122
Training Ground: Sheffield Wednesday Football Club Training Ground, Middlewood Road, Sheffield, S6 4HA
Brief History: Founded 1867 as The Wednesday F.C. (changed to Sheffield Wednesday c1930). Former Grounds: London Road, Wyrtle Road (Heeley), Sheaf House Ground, Endcliffe & Olive Grove (Bramall Lane also used occasionally), moved to Hillsborough (then named 'Owlerton') in 1899. Founder-members Second Division (1892). Record attendance 72,841
(Total) Current Capacity: 39,812 (all seated)
Visiting Supporters' Allocation: 3,700 (all seated) in West Stand Upper
Nearest Railway Station: Sheffield (2 miles)
Parking (Car): Street Parking
Parking (Coach/Bus): Owlerton Stadium
Police Force and Tel No: South Yorkshire (0114 220 2020)
Disabled Visitors' Facilities:
Wheelchairs: North and Lower West Stands
Blind: Commentary available
Anticipated Development(s): Towards the end of August 2009, the club announced plans for a £22million revamp of Hillsborough in order to raise the ground's capacity to 44,800 in the hope that the ground would be selected (as it was) as one of those for 2018 should England's bid for the World Cup be successful. The proposed work, for which formal permission was granted in the autumn of 2009, will see the extension of the North Stand as well as new roofs over the Kop and West stands along with the removal of internal pillars. If all goes according to schedule the work will be completed in 2013.

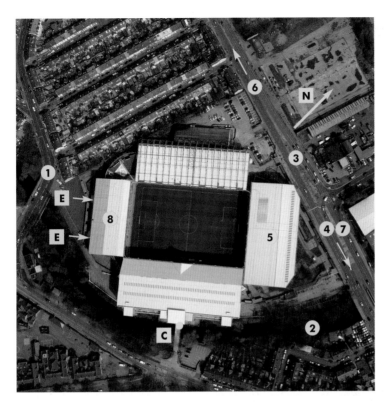

C Club Offices
E Entrance(s) for visiting
   supporters

1 Leppings Lane
2 River Don
3 A61 Penistone Road North
4 Sheffield station and
   City Centre (2 miles)
5 East Stand (Spion Kop)
6 To M1 (North)
7 To M1 (South)
8 West Stand

↑ North direction (approx)

◀ 701078
▼ 701082

shrewsbury town

Greenhous Meadow, Oteley Road, Shrewsbury, SY2 6ST

website: **WWW.SHREWSBURYTOWN.COM**
e:mail: **IAN@SHREWSBURYTOWN.CO.UK**
tel no: **01743 289177**
colours: **BLUE SHIRTS, WHITE SHORTS**
nickname: **THE SHREWS**
season 2010/11: **LEAGUE TWO**

Last Season: **12th** (p**46**; w**17**; d**12**; l**17**; gf**55**; ga**54**)

Although losing several notable players during the close season – most notably Ben Davies to Notts County and Grant Holt to Norwich City (both of whom ironically achieved promotion with their new teams) – hopes were high that Paul Simpson's Shrews would again be in the mix for the Play-Offs at the very least. Although suffering the aberration of a 1-0 home defeat to non-League Staines Town in the first round of the FA Cup, the Shrews' League form was such that a place in the Play-Offs looked a near certainty until a late loss of form following the 1-0 home victory over promotion-chasing Bournemouth – which left the team in sixth place – saw the team slip out of contention. A run of six straight defeats – including a 2-0 home defeat by doomed Darlington (a result that led Simpson to complain vocally about the attitude of some of the team's supporters) – and only three victories in the final 15 League matches consigned the Shrews to a position of mid-table mediocrity. With the Play-Offs a virtual impossibility, Simpson was sacked at the end of April, shortly before the final home game of the campaign. New boss Graham Turner (making his return to the club) will inherit a team that will undoubtedly need some remodelling. An ambitious club, it's likely that the Shrews will again be seen as candidates for automatic promotion and the Play-Offs in 2010/11.

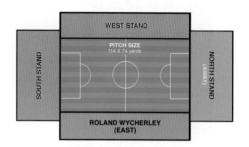

Advance Tickets Tel No: 01743 273943
Fax: 01743 246972
Training Ground: Sundorne Castle Training Ground, Newport Road, Sundorne, Shrewsbury SY1 4RR
Brief History: Founded 1886. Former Grounds: Monkmoor Racecourse, Ambler's Field; The Barracks Ground and the Gay Meadow (1910-2007); moved to the new ground for start of 2007/08 season. Elected to Football League 1950; relegated to Nationwide Conference at end of 2002/03 and promoted back to the Football League, via the Play-Offs, at the end of 2003/04. Record attendance at the Gay Meadow 18,917; at the New Stadium 8,753
(Total) Current Capacity: 9,875 (all seated)
Visiting Supporters' Allocation: tbc (North Stand)
Nearest Railway Station: Shrewsbury (two miles)
Parking (Car): at ground
Parking (Coach/Bus): at ground
Police Force and Tel No: West Mercia (0300 333 3000)
Disabled Visitors' Facilities:
Wheelchairs: c40 spaces in North (away), South and East stands
Blind: Commentary available
Anticipated Development(s): The ground was originally designed to permit the construction of corner infill accommodation to take the ground's total capacity to 12,500. Work on this development was scheduled to start in the summer of 2009, but has yet to commence.

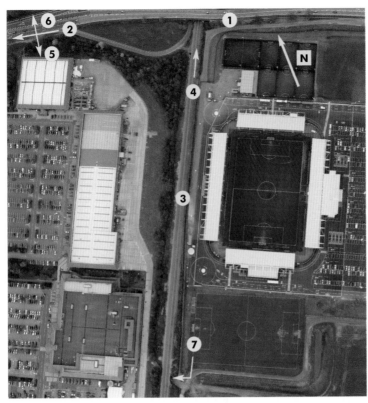

1 B4380 Oteley Road
2 Meole Brace roundabout
3 Shrewsbury-Hereford railway line
4 To Shrewsbury station (two miles)
5 A5112 Hereford Road to A5 (ring road)
6 A5191 Hereford Road to town centre and railway station
7 Footpath under railway to retail park

↑ North direction (approx)

◄ 701114
▼ 701118

southampton

St Mary's Stadium, Britannia Road, Southampton, SO14 5FP

website: **WWW.SAINTSFC.CO.UK**
e:mail: **SFC@SAINTSFC.CO.UK**
tel no: **0845 688 9448**
colours: **RED AND WHITE SHIRTS, BLACK SHORTS**
nickname: **THE SAINTS**
season 2010/11: **LEAGUE ONE**

Last Season: **7th*** (p**46**; w**23**; d**14**; l**9**; gf**85**; ga**47**)

Forced to start the 2009/10 season with a 10-point deduction as a result of going into Administration, Southampton passed into Swiss ownership in July 2009. With new funding in place, Saints made an impressive attempt at trying to defy the handicap of the point deduction. An indication of the progress being made on the field was shown by the club's 2-1 home victory over Roy Keane's Ipswich Town in the fourth round of the FA Cup. Finishing just outside the Play-Offs will be seen as a considerable success for Alan Pardew's side and will lay the foundation for a much more sustained attempt at both the Play-Offs and automatic promotion in 2010/11. It will be a considerable surprise if Saints don't maintain their on-field progress in the new season and the team ought undoubtedly to be in the mix for the top six places come May 2011.

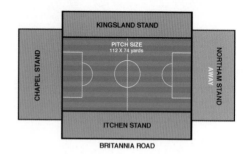

Advance Tickets Tel No: 0845 688 9288
Fax: 0845 688 9445
Training Ground: Staplewood, Club House, Long Lane, Marchwood, Southampton SO40 4WR
Brief History: Founded 1885 as 'Southampton St. Mary's Young Men's Association (changed name to Southampton in 1897). Former Grounds: Northlands Road, Antelope Ground, County Ground, moved to The Dell in 1898 and to St Mary's Stadium in 2001. Founder members Third Division (1920). Record attendance (at The Dell) 31,044; (at St Mary's) 32,151

(Total) Current Capacity: 32,689 (all seated)
Visiting Supporters' Allocation: c3,200 in Northam Stand (can be increased to 4,750 if required)
Nearest Railway Station: Southampton Central
Parking (Car): Street parking or town centre car parks
Parking (Coach/Bus): As directed by the police
Police Force and Tel No: Hampshire (02380 335444)
Disabled Visitors' Facilities:
Wheelchairs: c200 places
Blind: Commentary available

* Started the season with a 10-point deduction as a result of going into Administration.

C Club Offices
S Club Shop
E Entrance(s) for visiting
supporters

1 A3024 Northam Road
2 B3028 Britannia Road
3 River Itchen
4 To M27 (five miles)
5 To Southampton Central
station and town centre (one
mile)
6 Marine Parade
7 To A3025 (and Itchen
toll bridge)
8 Belvedere Road
9 Northam Stand

↑ North direction (approx)

◄ 703117
▼ 703121

southend united

Roots Hall Ground, Victoria Avenue, Southend-on-Sea, SS2 6NQ

website: **WWW.SOUTHENDUNITED.CO.UK**
e:mail: **INFO@SOUTHEND-UNITED.CO.UK**
tel no: **01702 304050**
colours: **BLUE SHIRTS, BLUE SHORTS**
nickname: **THE SHRIMPERS**
season 2010/11: **LEAGUE TWO**

Last Season: **23rd** (relegated) (p**46**; w**10**; d**13**; l**23**; gf**51**; ga**72**)

Having just missed the Play-Offs at the end of the 2008/09 season, hopes were high at Roots Hall that Steve Tilson's team would make a serious bid to reclaim a place in the Championship. However, problems both on and off the field conspired to see the club thankful to survive at all. Off the field, the Shrimpers were one of a number of clubs who seemed to be making almost as many court appearances as football fixtures as HMRC sought to claim outstanding taxes due. It was only in early April that the very real threat of a winding-up order was lifted. In terms of performances on the field, at the end of December the club was in a mid-table position but winning only four of the final 29 League matches saw the team drift down the table and relegation back to League Two was confirmed following the 2-2 draw away at Oldham Athletic. As a relegated team, United should be one of the teams that vie for the Play-Offs at the very least but it's difficult to estimate the impact that the financial problems of 2009/10 may have on strengthening the squad for the new season, Realistically, a top-half finish is perhaps the best that can be hoped for. The new season will see the team under Paul Sturrock as Steve Tilson was relieved of his duties in early July.

Advance Tickets Tel No: 0844 477 0077
Fax: 01702 304124
Training Ground: Eastern Avenue, Southend-on-Sea SS2 4DX
Brief History: Founded 1906. Former Grounds: Roots Hall, Kursaal, the Stadium Grainger Road, moved to Roots Hall (new Ground) 1955. Founder-members Third Division (1920). Record attendance 31,033
(Total) Current Capacity: 12,392 (all seated)
Visiting Supporters' Allocation: 2,000 (maximum) (all seated) in North Stand and North West Enclosure
Nearest Railway Station: Prittlewell
Parking (Car): Street parking
Parking (Coach/Bus): Car park at Ground
Police Force and Tel No: Essex (0300 333 4444)
Disabled Visitors' Facilities:
Wheelchairs: West Stand
Blind: Commentary available
Anticipated Development(s): The club submitted a proposal for the construction of its new £25 million 22,000-seat ground at Fossetts Farm to the council in early October 2006 and formal consent was granted by the council in January 2007 although this was subject to a public inquiry. Formal approval for the work was granted in March 2008. Final consent for the new ground was given by the government in July 2008. Funding for the work will come in part from the sale of Roots Hall to Sainsbury's for the construction of a new supermarket. The club hopes that work on the new ground, designed by HOK (who also designed the Emirates Stadium), will start in the summer of 2010 with the intention that the new ground will be completed for the start of the 2012/13 season.

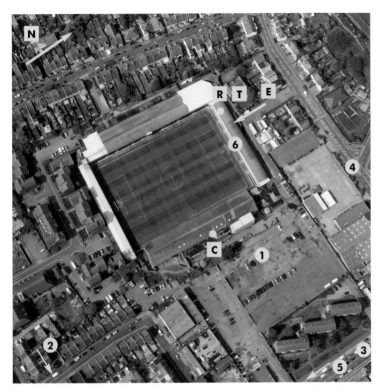

C Club Offices
E Entrance(s) for visiting
   supporters
R Refreshment bars for visiting
   supporters
T Toilets for visiting supporters

1 Director's Car Park
2 Prittlewell station
   (¼ mile)
3 A127 Victoria Aveneue
4 Fairfax Drive
5 Southend centre (½ mile)
6 North (Universal Cycles)
   Stand

↑ North direction (approx)

◄ 702417
▼ 702451

stevenage

The Lamex Stadium, Broadhall Way, Stevenage, Hertfordshire SG2 8RH

web Site: **WWW.STEVENAGEBOROFC.COM**
e-mail: **ROGERA@ STEVENAGEBOROFC.COM**
tel no: **01438 223223**
colours: **WHITE SHIRTS, RED SHORTS**
nickname: **BORO**
season 2010/11: **LEAGUE TWO**

Last Season: **1st** (promoted) (p**44**; w**30**; d**9**; l**5**; gf**79**; ga**24**)

A member of the Conference in its various guises since winning promotion from the Diadora (Isthmian) Premier League at the end of the 1993/94 season, Stevenage Borough finally achieved promotion to the Football League at the end of the 2009/10 season, 14 years after the club had first finished top. Unfortunately, at the end of the 1995/96 season, the club's ground was deemed unsuitable for the League and so the club remained outside the Football League. For much of the 2009/10 season it looked as though Oxford United were going to be the team to achieve automatic promotion but under Graham Westley, manager (for the second time at the club) from May 2008, Boro's end of season run saw the team ultimately pip Luton Town to the top spot in the penultimate game of the season. A 1-0 victory at Kidderminster Harriers in mid-April ensured that League football would be played at Broadhall Way for the first time in 2010/11. As a team promoted from the Conference, Boro will need first to establish itself at the higher level, but in recent years teams promoted from the Conference – such as Aldershot and Burton Albion – have prospered and Stevenage should be well capable of at least a mid-table position.

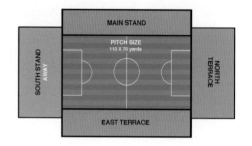

Advance Tickets Tel No: 01438 223223
Fax: 01438 743666
Training Ground: Stevenage Borough Football Academy, Shephallbury Sports Centre, Broadhall Way, Stevenage SG2 8RH

Brief History: The club was founded in 1976 when it replaced the earlier club Stevenage Athletic that had gone bankrupt. Initially the new club played at the town's King George V playing fields before returning to the old Athletic ground at Broadhall Way in 1980 and adopting the suffix 'Borough'. The suffix has been dropped now that League status has been gained. Record attendance (at Broadhall Way) 8,040

(Total) Current Capacity: 7,100 (3,412 seated)
Visiting Supporters' Allocation: 1,400 (all seated) (South Stand)
Nearest Railway Station: Stevenage (one mile)
Parking (Car): A large car park is available on the A4602 across the road from the Lamex Stadium
Parking (Coach/Bus): As directed
Police Force and Tel No: Hertfordshire Constabulary (0345 3300 222)
Disabled Visitors' Facilities:
Wheelchairs: 12 allocated spaces for home and away fans located at the rear of the North Terrace
Blind: No special facility
Anticipated Development(s):

1 A602 Broadhall Way
2 B197 Monkswood Way
3 To M1 Junction 7
4 To Stevenage station and town centre
5 A602 to Watton-at-Stone
6 North Terrace
7 South Stand (away)
8 Main Stand
9 East Terrace

↑ North direction (approx)

◄ 703212
▼ 703215

stockport county

Edgeley Park, Hardcastle Road, Edgeley, Stockport, SK3 9DD

website: **WWW.STOCKPORTCOUNTY.COM**
e:mail: **FANS@STOCKPORTCOUNTY.COM**
tel no: **0161 286 8888**
colours: **BLUE STRIPE SHIRTS, BLUE SHORTS**
nickname: **THE HATTERS**
season 2010/11: **LEAGUE TWO**

Last Season: **24th** (relegated) (**p46**; w**5**; d**10**; l**31**; gf**35**; ga**95**)

With the club entering Administration towards the end of the 2008/09 season, the new campaign under Gary Ablett, appointed manager at Edgeley Park during the close season, was always going to be a struggle. The reality from the start of the season was that the club struggled to make an impact in League One. Although the season started reasonably well, with the club in mid-table, a run of nine League defeats – plus the FA Cup loss 4-0 to League Two side Torquay United in the second round of the FA Cup (in a match played in mid-December at Macclesfield Town's ground) – saw the team plummet to the bottom of the table, with a significant point difference between the team and safely. The club was never to recover from this and relegation to League Two was confirmed following the home defeat against Yeovil Town in early April. With the club still in Administration, although there are hopes that a buyer will come along during the close season, County will enter League Two at a considerable disadvantage. Unless the position is resolved quickly, it's hard to escape the conclusion that 2010/11 will again prove to be a struggle and survival could once more be the name of the game. In mid-June it was announced that Ablett had left the club with Paul Simpson appointed in mid-July.

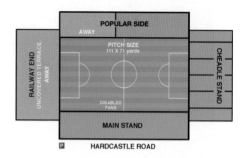

Advance Tickets Tel No: 0845 688 5799
Fax: 0161 429 7392
Training Ground: Details omitted at club's request
Brief History: Founded 1883 as Heaton Norris Rovers, changed name to Stockport County in 1890. Former Grounds: Heaton Norris Recreation Ground, Heaton Norris Wanderers Cricket Ground, Chorlton's Farm, Ash Inn Ground, Wilkes Field (Belmont Street) and Nursery Inn (Green Lane), moved to Edgeley Park in 1902. Record attendance 27,833
(Total) Current Capacity: 10,650 (all seated)
Visiting Supporters' Allocation: 1,558 (all-seated) on the open Railway End plus 800 seats, if required, on Popular Side
Nearest Railway Station: Stockport
Parking (Car): Street Parking
Parking (Coach/Bus): As directed by Police
Other Clubs Sharing Ground: Sale Sharks RUFC
Police Force and Tel No: Greater Manchester (0161 872 5050)
Disabled Visitors' Facilities:
Wheelchairs: Main and Cheadle stands
Blind: Headsets available
Anticipated Development(s): Although the club is still planning for the reconstruction of the Railway End, with the intention of constructing a new 5,500-seat capacity stand on the site, there is no time scale for this work (which had originally been planned for 1999/2000). Theoretically, the next phase after the Railway End would be an upgrade to the Vernon BS Stand, with the intention of making the ground's capacity 20,000.

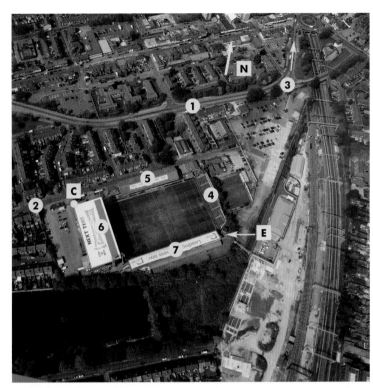

C Club Offices
E Entrance(s) for visiting
   supporters

1 Mercian Way
2 Hardcastle Road
3 Stockport station
   (¼ mile)
4 Railway End
5 Main Stand
6 Cheadle Stand
7 Main Stand

↑ North direction (approx)

◄ 701279
▼ 701273

stoke city

Britannia Stadium, Stanley Matthews Way, Stoke-on-Trent, ST4 4EG

website: **WWW.STOKECITYFC.COM**
e:mail: **INFO@STOKECITYFC.COM**
tel no: **0871 663 2008**
colours: **RED AND WHITE STRIPED SHIRTS, WHITE SHORTS**
nickname: **THE POTTERS**
season 2010/11: **PREMIER LEAGUE**

Having survived one season in the Premier League, there was always a danger that Tony Pulis's Stoke City could suffer from a severe bout of 'second-seasonitis' but, unlike Hull City, the Potters performed sufficiently well to ensure both that safety was ensured well before the end of the season and that a position of mid-table security was achieved. One concern for fans is that home form has been less secure than in 2008/09. For 2010/11, with arguably at last two strong teams coming up in West Brom and Newcastle United, City could face a more serious challenge to the club's Premier League status in the new season.

Last Season: **11th** (p**38**; w**11**; d**14**; l**13**; gf**34**; ga**48**)

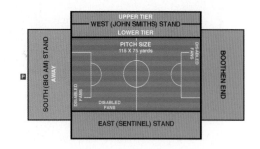

Advance Tickets Tel No: 0871 663 2008
Fax: 01782 592 210

Training Ground: Clayton Wood Training Ground, Rosetree Avenue, Trent Vale, Stoke-on-Trent ST4 6NL

Brief History: Founded 1863 as Stoke F.C., amalgamated with Stoke Victoria in 1878, changed to Stoke City in 1925. Former Grounds: Sweetings Field, Victoria Ground (1878-1997), moved to new ground for start of 1997/98 season. Record attendance (at Victoria Ground): 51,380; at Britannia Stadium 28,218

(Total) Current Capacity: 28,383 (all seated)

Visiting Supporters' Allocation: 2,800 (in the South Stand)

Nearest Railway Station: Stoke-on-Trent

Parking (Car): The 650 parking spaces at the ground are for officials and guests only. The 1,600 spaces in the South car park are pre-booked only, with the majority held by season ticket holders. There is some on-street parking, but with a 10-15min walk.

Parking (Coach/Bus): As directed

Police Force and Tel No: Staffordshire (0300 123 4455)

Disabled Visitors' Facilities:
Wheelchairs: 164 places for disabled spectators
Blind: Commentaries available

Anticipated Development(s): There are long-term plans to increase the ground's capacity to 30,000 by the construction of a corner stand between the John Smith Stand and the Boothen End but there is no timescale for this work.

1 A50
2 To Stoke station
3 To A500 Queensway and City Centre, railway station and M6
4 North (Boothen End) Stand
5 West (John Smith's) Stand
6 East (Sentinel) Stand
7 South (Big AM) Stand (away)
8 To Uttoxeter
9 Stanley Matthews Way

↑ *North direction (approx)*

◄ 703088
▼ 703099

sunderland

Stadium of Light, Sunderland SR5 1SU

website: **WWW.SAFC.COM**
e:mail: **ENQUIRIES@SAFC.COM**
tel no: **0871 911 1200**
colours: **RED AND WHITE STRIPED SHIRTS, BLACK SHORTS**
nickname: **THE BLACK CATS**
season 2010/11: **PREMIER LEAGUE**

Last Season: **13th** (p**38**; w**11** d**11**; l**16**; gf**48**; ga**56**)

Appointed during the close season in 2009, Steve Bruce enjoyed a promising start to his first season in charge of the Black Cats, seeing Sunderland initially challenging for a place in the Europa League positions. Amongst the early-season victories was a 1-0 victory at the Stadium of Light over Liverpool where the 'assist' came from a most unlikely source – an errant beach ball in the penalty area that diverted the match ball past the Liverpool keeper. Unfortunately, Sunderland's luck didn't hold for long and results in mid-season saw the team gradually drift down the Premier League table. Although always just out of the real relegation battle, there must have been occasions during the latter part of the season when Sunderland fans peered nervously at the table as the teams below them gradually garnered points. In the event, however, Sunderland survived comfortably and should probably be considered as one of the teams secure in the Premier League's mid-table division: not strong enough to sustain a challenge for the top places over the season but not weak enough to be dragged down into the relegation mire. Provided that Bruce can retain his key players and recruit judiciously in the close season, a top-half finish is possible.

Advance Tickets Tel No: 0871 911 1973
Fax: 0191 551 5123
Training Ground: The Academy of Light, Sunderland Road, Sunderland SR6 7UN
Brief History: Founded 1879 as 'Sunderland & District Teachers Association', changed to 'Sunderland Association' in 1880 and shortly after to 'Sunderland'. Former Grounds: Blue House Field, Groves Field (Ashbrooke), Horatio Street, Abbs Field, Newcastle Road and Roker Park (1898-1997); moved to Stadium of Light for the start of the 1997/98 season. Record crowd (at Roker Park): 75,118; (at Stadium of Light) 48,353
(Total) Current Capacity: 49,000 (all seated)
Visiting Supporters' Allocation: 3,000 (South Stand)
Nearest Railway Station: Stadium of Light (Tyne & Wear Metro)
Parking (Car): Car park at ground reserved for season ticket holders. Limited on-street parking (but the police may decide to introduce restrictions). Otherwise off-street parking in city centre
Parking (Coach/Bus): As directed
Police Force and Tel No: Northumbria (0345 604 3043)
Disabled Visitors' Facilities:
Wheelchairs: 180 spots
Blind: Commentary available
Anticipated Development(s): The club has planning permission to increase capacity at the Stadium of Light by 7,200 in an expanded Metro FM Stand and plans a further 9,000 in a second tier to the McEwans Stand, taking the ultimate capacity of the ground to 64,000. There is, however, no confirmed timescale.

C Club Offices
S Club Shop
E Entrance(s) for visiting
   supporters

1 River Wear
2 North (Kronenburg) Stand
3 South (Metro FM) Stand
   (away)
4 To Sunderland station
   (¹/₂ mile)
5 Southwick Road
6 Stadium Way
7 Millennium Way
8 May Street
9 To Wearmouth Bridge (via
   A1018 North Bridge Street)
   to City Centre

↑ North direction (approx)

◄ 701290
▼ 701284

swansea city

Liberty Stadium, Morfa, Swansea SA1 2FA

website: **WWW.SWANSEACITY.NET**
e:mail: **INFO@SWANSEACITYFC.CO.UK**
tel no: **01792 616600**
colours: **WHITE SHIRTS, BLACK SHORTS**
nickname: **THE SWANS**
season 2010/11: **CHAMPIONSHIP**

Last Season: **7th** (p**46**; w**17**; d**14**; l**15**; gf**40**; ga**37**)

A case of 'so near, yet so far' for the now-departed Paulo Sousa's Swansea City as the club seemed assured of a Play-Off place at the very least for much of the campaign. As late as early March, the club was in fourth place some nine points ahead of Blackpool – ironically the team that was to achieve promotion to the Premier League through the Play-Offs – in seventh place with only 11 League fixtures left. However, a late loss of form that saw the Swans win only two of the club's last 11 League fixtures saw the team gradually slip down the Championship table although mathematically the club retained a chance of achieving the Play-Offs through to the final Sunday of the season. Needing to better Blackpool's result, Swansea's 0-0 draw at home against Doncaster allied to Blackpool's draw against Bristol City meant that the Swans lost out and thus face another season in the Championship. With two of the relegated teams from the Premier League looking financially weaker than usual and thus posing perhaps less of a challenge to existing Championship teams, City under Brendon Rodgers ought to have the potential once again in 2010/11 to mount a challenge for the Play-Offs at least.

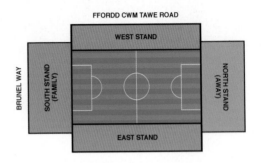

Advance Tickets Tel No: 0870 400004
Fax: 01792 616606
Training Ground: Llandarcy Academy of Sport, Neath SA10 6JD
Brief History: Founded 1900 as Swansea Town, changed to Swansea City in 1970. Former grounds: various, including Recreation Ground, and Vetch Field (1912-2005); moved to the new ground for the start of the 2005/06 season. Founder-members Third Division (1920). Record attendance (at Vetch Field): 32,796; (at Liberty Stadium) 19,288.
(Total) Current Capacity: 20,500 (all seated)
Visiting Supporters' Allocation: 3,500 maximum in North Stand
Nearest Railway Station: Swansea
Parking (Car): Adjacent to ground
Parking (Coach/Bus): As directed
Other Clubs Sharing Ground: Swansea Ospreys RUFC
Police Force and Tel No: South Wales (01656 655555)
Disabled Visitors' Facilities:
Wheelchairs: 252 spaces
Blind: No special facility
Anticipated Development(s): After several years of uncertainty, Swansea City relocated to the new Liberty Stadium with its 20,000 all-seater capacity for the start of the 2005/06 season. The ground, which cost £27 million to construct and which was built near the site of the old Morfa stadium, is shared by the Swansea Ospreys RUFC team.

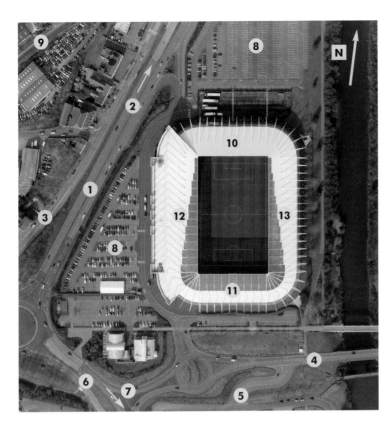

◀ 702828
▼ 702831

167

swindon town

County Ground, County Road, Swindon, SN1 2ED

website: **WWW.SWINDONTOWNFC.CO.UK**
e:mail: **ENQUIRIES@SWINDONTOWNFC.CO.UK**
tel no: **0871 423 6433**
colours: **RED SHIRTS, RED SHORTS**
nickname: **THE ROBINS**
season 2010/11: **LEAGUE ONE**

Last Season: **5th (p46; w22; d16; l8; gf73; ga57)**

A poor start to the season saw Danny Wilson, in his first full season in control at the County Ground, and his team struggle initially as the team battled to move up from mid-table. As the season progressed, however, the team's performances improved; the club gradually ascended the League One table and started to make a serious push for the second automatic promotion place – aided and abetted, it has to be said, by the decline in Leeds United's form during the second half of the season. Come the final Saturday of the campaign, Swindon were one of five teams with a mathematical chance of achieving the second promotion spot behind champions Norwich City. However, the Robins faced a tricky away match at promotion rivals Millwall. A 3-2 defeat consigned the club to the Play-Offs. In the Play-Offs, Town faced Charlton Athletic and, with the aggregate score tied at 3-3 after extra time, Swindon triumphed on penalties. In the Wembley final Town again faced Millwall with the Londoners once more coming out on top, winning 1-0 to ensure League One football is again on offer at the County Ground in 2010/11. Provided that the progress made on the field in 2009/10 is maintained in the new season, Swindon ought to be one of the teams challenging for the Play-Offs at least.

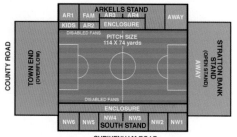

Advance Tickets Tel No: 0871 223 2300
Fax: 0844 880 1112
Training Ground: Zurich, Wanborough, Swindon SN4 0DY
Brief History: Founded 1881. Former Grounds: Quarry Ground, Globe Road, Croft Ground, County Ground (adjacent to current Ground and now Cricket Ground), moved to current County Ground in 1896. Founder-members Third Division (1920). Record attendance 32,000
(Total) Current Capacity: 15,728 (all seated)
Visiting Supporters' Allocation: 3,342 (all seated) maximum in Arkell's Stand and Stratton Bank (open)
Nearest Railway Station: Swindon
Parking (Car): Town Centre
Parking (Coach/Bus): Adjacent car park
Police Force and Tel No: Wiltshire (0845 408 7000)
Disabled Visitors' Facilities:
Wheelchairs: In front of Arkell's Stand
Blind: Commentary available
Anticipated Development(s): In late 2008 Town's chairman announced that the club would now seek to redevelop the County Ground rather than relocate.

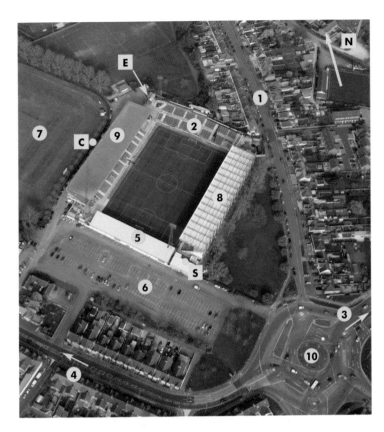

C Club Offices
S Club Shop
E Entrance(s) for visiting
 supporters

1 Shrivenham Road
2 Stratton Bank (away)
3 A345 Queens Drive
 (M4 Junction 15 –
 3½ miles)
4 To Swindon station
 (½ mile)
5 Town End
6 Car Park
7 County Cricket Ground
8 Don Rogers Stand
9 Arkell's Stand
10 'Magic' Roundabout

↑ North direction (approx)

◄ 702352
▾ 702372

torquay united

Plainmoor, Torquay TQ1 3PS

web Site: **WWW.TORQUAYUNITED.COM**
e:mail: **RECEPTION@TORQUAYUNITED.COM**
tel no: **01803 328666**
colours: **YELLOW AND BLUE SHIRTS, YELLOW SHORTS**
nickname: **THE GULLS**
season 2010/11: **LEAGUE TWO**

Last Season: **17th** (p**46**; w**14**; d**15**; l**17**; gf**64**; ga**55**)

Promoted through the Play-Offs at the end of the 2008/09 season, Paul Buckle's Torquay United team faced the challenge of re-establishing the club as a League team after an absence of several years. For much of the campaign it looked as though the Gulls were going to be grateful that, in Darlington and Grimsby, League Two possessed two teams that seemed considerably weaker than the remainder of the division as the club hovered just above the drop zone. However, a late burst of form, which saw the team win six and draw two of its last eight League fixtures, saw the team ultimately finish in a secure and creditable 17th place some 13 points above relegated Grimsby. Away from the League, the club also triumphed 4-0 away at League One strugglers Stockport County in the 2nd round of the FA Cup. Provided that the momentum that the team showed towards the back end of the 2009/10 season is maintained, then a top-half finish for 2010/11 is possible but the reality is that the club will again probably finish in the lower half of the table.

Advance Tickets Tel No: 01803 328666
Fax: 01803 323976
Training Ground: Old Seale Hayne Campus, Howton Lane, TQ12 6NQ
Brief History: Founded 1898 as Torquay United, amalgamated with Ellacombe in 1910 and name changed to Torquay Town. Amalgamated with Babbacombe in 1921 and name changed to Torquay United. Former Grounds: Teignmouth Road, Torquay Road, Cricketfield Road and Torquay Cricket Ground, moved to Plainmoor (Ellacombe's ground) in 1910. Relegated to the Conference in 2006/07 and promoted back to the Football League in 2008/09. Record attendance 21,908
(Total) Current Capacity: 6,283 (2,446 seated)
Visiting Supporters' Allocation: 1,100 (Sparkworld Away Stand) plus 200 seats (Main Stand)
Nearest Railway Station: Torquay (two miles)
Parking (Car): Street parking
Parking (Coach/Bus): Lymington Road coach station
Police Force and Tel No: Devon & Cornwall (08452 777444)
Disabled Visitors' Facilities:
Wheelchairs: Ellacombe End
Blind: No specific facility
Anticipated Development(s): The club has plans for the redevelopment of the Main Stand into a new 2,500-seat structure although there is no timescale for the work at present.

C Club Offices
S Club Shop
E Entrance(s) for visiting
   supporters

1 Warbro Road
2 B3202 Marychurch Road
3 Marnham Road
4 To Torquay station
   (two miles)
5 To A38
6 Sparkworld Away Stand

↑ *North direction (approx)*

◄ 700394
▼ 700393

tottenham hotspur

White Hart Lane, Bill Nicholson Way, 748 High Road, Tottenham, London N17 0AP

website: **WWW.TOTTENHAMHOTSPUR.COM**
e:mail: **CUSTOMER.CARE@TOTTENHAMHOTSPUR.COM**
tel no: **0844 499 5000**
colours: **WHITE SHIRTS, NAVY BLUE SHORTS**
nickname: **SPURS**
season 2010/11: **PREMIER LEAGUE**

Last Season: **4th** (p**38**; w**21**; d**7**; l**10**; gf**67**; ga**41**)

Although no silverware arrived at White Hart Lane at the end of the 2009/10 season, Harry Redknapp and his Tottenham team can look back on the last season as one of considerable success, given that Spurs finally broke the domination of the top-four places and, in finishing fourth, brought the team entry into the qualifying rounds of the Champions League for the first time. Some impressive League performances during the season – including the 9-1 home thrashing of Wigan Athletic – and a good run in the FA Cup, where the team reached the semi-finals before surprisingly losing 2-0 to Portsmouth were capped by the thrill of the 1-0 victory at the City of Manchester Stadium over Manchester City, which ensured Spurs' entry into the Champions League at the expense of their free-spending hosts. There were occasional glitches during the season, such as the 1-0 home defeat by Wolves, but overall fans will be pleased with progress. The challenge for 2010/11 will be to sustain the grip on the Champions League places, particularly given the ambition of Manchester City, whilst competing both at home and in Europe. Harry Redknapp has proved himself adept at getting the maximum out of his squad and, with strengthening over the summer, Spurs should again be one of the teams chasing a top-four berth although the club's best route to silverware may well come in one of the domestic cup competitions.

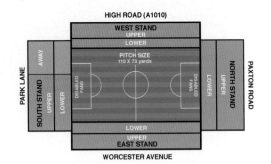

Ticket Line: 0844 844 0102
Fax: 020 8365 5005
Training Ground: Spurs Lodge, Luxborough Lane, Chigwell IG7 5AB
Brief History: Founded 1882 as 'Hotspur', changed name to Tottenham Hotspur in 1885. Former Grounds: Tottenham Marshes and Northumberland Park, moved to White Hart Lane in 1899. F.A. Cup winner 1901 (as a non-League club). Record attendance 75,038
(Total) Current Capacity: 36,257 (all seated)
Visiting Supporters' Allocation: 3,000
(in South and West Stands)
Nearest Railway Station: White Hart Lane plus Seven Sisters and Manor House (tube)
Parking (Car): Street parking (min ¼ mile from ground)
Parking (Coach/Bus): Northumberland Park coach park
Police Force and Tel No: Metropolitan (0300 123 1212)
Disabled Visitors' Facilities:
Wheelchairs: North and South Stands (by prior arrangement)
Blind: Commentary available
Anticipated Development(s): The club submitted its planning application for the construction of a new 56,250-seat ground, to be built adjacent to the existing ground, to the local authority in October 2009. If all goes according to plan, the club intends to move to the partially completed new ground for the start of the 2012/13 season with work being completed for the start of the following season. The application also covered the construction of 434 new homes on the site of the old ground, a 150-bed hotel and a supermarket.

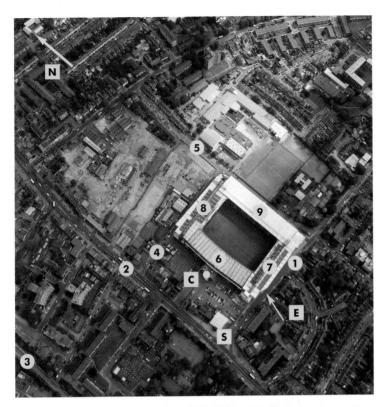

C Club Offices
S Club Shop
E Entrance(s) for visiting
   supporters

1 Park Lane
2 A1010 High Road
3 White Hart Lane station
4 Paxton Road
5 Worcester Avenue
6 West Stand
7 South Stand
8 North Stand
9 East Stand

↑ North direction (approx)

◄ 703200
▼ 703202

tranmere rovers

Prenton Park, Prenton Road West, Birkenhead, CH42 9PY

website: **WWW.TRANMEREROVERS.CO.UK**
e:mail: **INFO@TRANMEREROVERS.CO.UK**
tel no: **0871 221 2001**
colours: **WHITE SHIRTS, WHITE SHORTS**
nickname: **ROVERS**
season 2010/11: **LEAGUE ONE**

Last Season: **19th** (p**46**; w**14**; d**9**; l**23**; gf**45**; ga**72**)

Although only appointed in July 2009, John Barnes's tenure of the manager's job at Prenton Park was to be short as he and assistant Jason McAteer were sacked in early October following a poor start to the season. Two wins out of the club's first 11 League matches, culminating in a 5-0 drubbing by Millwall that left the team in 22nd place, sealed Barnes's fate. The club moved quickly to make Les Parry, who'd been the team's physiotherapist for almost two decades, to the post of caretaker and, in mid-December, following a run of five wins and three draws in League and FA Cup matches, the appointment was made permanent until the end of the season. At this stage the club was still deep in the drop zone, a position that remained the case until a late run of three wins and a draw in the final five League matches saw the team survive the drop by a single point, although safety wasn't ensured until the final day of the season. A 3-0 away victory over already relegated Stockport combined with results elsewhere ensured that Rovers survived in League One for another season. For 2010/11 the manager will need to strengthen the squad otherwise a further battle to avoid the drop looks likely.

Advance Tickets Tel No: 0871 221 2001
Fax: 0151 609 0606
Training Ground: Raby Vale, Willaston Road, Clatterbridge CH63 4JG
Brief History: Founded 1884 as Belmont F.C., changed name to Tranmere Rovers in 1885 (not connected to earlier 'Tranmere Rovers'). Former grounds: Steele's Field and Ravenshaw's Field (also known as Old Prenton Park, ground of Tranmere Rugby Club), moved to (new) Prenton Park in 1911. Founder-members 3rd Division North (1921). Record attendance 24,424.
(Total) Current Capacity: 16,587 (all seated)
Visiting Supporters' Allocation: 2,500 (all-seated) in Cow Shed Stand
Nearest Railway Station: Hamilton Square or Rock Ferry
Parking (Car): Car park at Ground
Parking (Coach/Bus): Car park at Ground
Other Clubs Sharing Ground: Liverpool Reserves
Police Force and Tel No: Merseyside (0151 709 6010)
Disabled Visitors' Facilities:
Wheelchairs: Main Stand
Blind: Commentary available

C Club Offices
S Club Shop
E Entrance(s) for visiting
supporters

1 Car Park
2 Prenton Road West
3 Borough Road
4 M53 Junction 4 (B5151) –
3 miles
5 Birkenhead (1 mile)
6 Cow Shed Stand
7 Kop Shed

↑ *North direction (approx)*

◂ 702200
▾ 702175

walsall

Banks's Stadium, Bescot Crescent, Walsall, West Midlands, WS1 4SA

website: **WWW.SADDLERS.CO.UK**
e:mail: **INFO@WALSALLFC.CO.UK**
tel no: **01922 622971**
colours: **RED SHIRTS, WHITE SHORTS**
nickname: **THE SADDLERS**
season 2010/11: **LEAGUE ONE**

Last Season: **10th** (p**46**; w**16**; d**14**;l**16**; gf**60**; ga**63**)

A poor start to the season, including a 2-1 defeat away at League Two Accrington Stanley in the 1st round of the Carling Cup, seemed to set the tempo for Chris Hutchings and his Walsall team. Never strong enough to mount a sustained challenge for the Play-Offs nor weak enough to be sucked into the relegation mire, the Saddlers performed as a mid-table team for much of the campaign. Results late in the season, however, with four wins in the club's final seven League matches, suggest that, with judicious strengthening, the club's fortunes for the new season might be brighter.

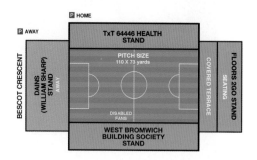

Advance Tickets Tel No: 01922 615414/416
Fax: 01922 613202
Training Ground: The Pavilion, Broad Lane, Essington, Wolverhampton WV11 2RH
Brief History: Founded 1888 as Walsall Town Swifts (amalgamation of Walsall Town – founded 1884 – and Walsall Swifts – founded 1885), changed name to Walsall in 1895. Former Grounds: The Chuckery, West Bromwich Road (twice), Hilary Street (later named Fellows Park, twice), moved to Bescot Stadium in 1990. Founder-members Second Division (1892). Record attendance 11,049 (25,453 at Fellows Park)
(Total) Current Capacity: 11,300 (all seated)
Visiting Supporters' Allocation: 2,000 maximum in Dains Stand
Nearest Railway Station: Bescot
Parking (Car): Car park at Ground
Parking (Coach/Bus): Car park at Ground
Police Force and Tel No: West Midlands (0345 113 5000)
Disabled Visitors' Facilities:
Wheelchairs: Banks's Stand
Blind: No special facility
Anticipated Development(s): Planning permission was granted in the summer of 2004 for the redevelopment of the William Sharp Stand to add a further 2,300 seats, taking the away allocation up to 4,000 and the total ground capacity to 13,500. The project is to be funded via advertising directed towards the adjacent M6 but work has yet to commence.

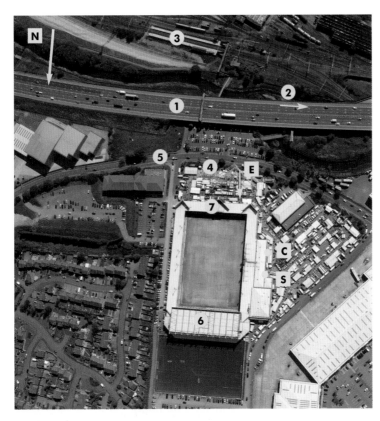

C Club Offices
S Club Shop
E Entrance(s) for visiting
   supporters

1 Motorway M6
2 M6 Junction 9
3 Bescot station
4 Car Parks
5 Bescot Crescent
6 Floors2Go (Gilbert Alsop)
   Stand
7 Dains (William Sharp) Stand
   (away)

↑ North direction (approx)

◄ 702570
▼ 702592

watford

Vicarage Road Stadium, Vicarage Road, Watford, WD18 0ER

website: **WWW.WATFORDFC.COM**
e:mail: **YOURVOICE@WATFORDFC.COM**
tel no: **0845 856 1881**
colours: **YELLOW SHIRTS, BLACK SHORTS**
nickname: **THE HORNETS**
season 2010/11: **CHAMPIONSHIP**

Last Season: **16th** (p**46**; w**14**; d**12**; l**20**; gf**61**; ga**68**)

A difficult first season for Malky Mackay as the Watford boss saw the team struggle in the Championship with relegation a very real threat on the field and Administration a possibility off it. Hovering just above the drop zone for much of the campaign, three wins in the club's last five League matches dragged the team away from the bottom three and resulted in the club finishing some seven points above relegated Sheffield Wednesday. Away from the League, the team was also defeated 2-1 by League One Leeds United at Elland Road in the 2nd round of the Carling Cup. For the future, the club has announced a fund-raising programme and life-president Elton John will also be holding a concert at Vicarage Road to raise funds, with the intention that the money generated will be used to strengthen the squad. Investment in the team will undoubtedly be necessary if the club is to avoid another battle against the drop but the probability is that the Hornets will probably continue to struggle at this level.

Advance Tickets Tel No: 0845 856 1881
Fax: 01923 496001
Training Ground: University College London Sports Grounds, Bell Lane, London Colney, St Albans AL2 1BZ
Brief History: Founded 1898 as an amalgamation of West Herts (founded 1891) and Watford St. Mary's (founded early 1890s). Former Grounds: Wiggenhall Road (Watford St. Mary's) and West Herts Sports Ground, moved to Vicarage Road in 1922. Founder-members Third Division (1920). Record attendance 34,099
(Total) current Capacity: 19,900 (all seated)
Visiting Supporters' Allocation: 2,200 – 4,500 maximum in Vicarage Road (North) Stand
Nearest Railway Station: Watford High Street or Watford Junction
Parking (Car): Nearby multi-storey car park in town centre (10 mins walk)
Parking (Coach/Bus): Cardiff Road car park
Other Clubs Sharing Ground: Saracens RUFC
Police Force and Tel No: Hertfordshire (0345 330 0222)
Disabled Visitors' Facilities:
Wheelchairs: Corner East Stand and South Stand (special enclosure for approx. 24 wheelchairs), plus enclosure in North East Corner
Blind: Commentary available in the East Stand (20 seats, free of charge)
Anticipated Development(s): Although planning consent for the redevelopment of the East Stand was obtained in early 2008, work on the demolition of the original stand was delayed and the ground's capacity reduced to 17,500 for the 2008/09 season. In order to fund part of the work key-worker accommodation is being built around the stadium – as illustrated in the photographs – in conjunction with the Oracle housing association. Once all work is completed, including the construction of the new East Stand and the infill of the corners the ground's capacity will be 23,000. If work goes to schedule it should be completed by the start of the 2011/12 season.

S Club Shop

1 Vicarage Road
2 Occupation Road
3 Rous Stand
4 Town Centre (½ mile) – Car Parks, High Street station
5 Vicarage Road Stand (away)
6 East Stand
7 Rookery End

↑ North direction (approx)

◄ 702897
▼ 702903

west bromwich albion

The Hawthorns, Halfords Lane, West Bromwich, West Midlands B71 4LF

website: **WWW.WBA.CO.UK**
e:mail: **ENQUIRIES@WBAFC.CO.UK**
tel no: **0871 271 1100**
colours: **NAVY BLUE AND WHITE STRIPED SHIRTS, WHITE SHORTS**
nickname: **THE BAGGIES**
season 2010/11: **PREMIER LEAGUE**

Relegated at the end of the 2008/09 season, West Brom was also faced by the loss of its manager when Tony Mowbray decided to take over as boss at Celtic. The Baggies moved quickly to appoint Roberto di Matteo, who'd proved successful with Milton Keynes Dons during the 2008/09 season, to the vacancy at The Hawthorns. Under di Matteo, the Baggies prospered and were always in the hunt for automatic promotion, although they were pushed by a resurgent Nottingham Forest until, shortly after Easter, when promotion back to the Premier League was again guaranteed. Thus West Brom's yo-yo existence continues. In recent years the assumption that promoted teams were automatic relegation fodder has been slightly misplaced; teams like Stoke and Birmingham have survived, although others – most notably last season Burnley – have flattered to deceive. Well run and with an astute manager, albeit untested at Premier League level, West Brom ought to have the potential to replicate Stoke's success but, as always, it will be a close thing and 17th place will undoubtedly be seen as a triumph.

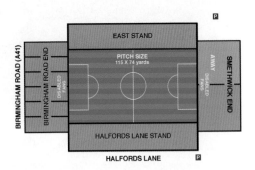

Advance Tickets Tel No: 0871 271 9780
Fax: 0871 271 9861
Training Ground: West Bromwich Albion FC Development Centre, 430 Birmingham Road, Walsall WS5 3LQ
Brief History: Founded 1879. Former Grounds: Coopers Hill, Dartmouth Park, Four Acres, Stoney Lane, moved to the Hawthorns in 1900. Founder-members of Football League (1888). Record attendance 64,815
(Total) Current Capacity: 28,000 (all seated)
Visiting Supporters' Allocation: 3,000 in Smethwick End (can be increased to 5,200 if required)
Nearest Railway Station: The Hawthorns
Parking (Car): Halfords Lane and Rainbow Stand car parks
Parking (Coach/Bus): Rainbow Stand car park
Police Force and Tel No: West Midlands (0345 113 5000)
Disabled Visitors' Facilities:
Wheelchairs: Apollo 2000 and Smethwick Road End
Blind: Facility available
Anticipated Development(s): The club has applied for planning permission to rebuild the area between the East Stand and Birmingham Road End to take capacity to 32,500.

C Club Offices
S Club Shop
E Entrance(s) for visiting
  supporters

1 A41 Birmingham Road
2 To M5 Junction 1
3 Birmingham Centre
  (4 miles)
4 Halfords Lane
5 Main (Halfords Lane) Stand
6 Smethwick End
7 Rolfe Street, Smethwick
  station (1½ miles)
8 To The Hawthorns station
9 East Stand
10 Birmingham Road End

⬆ North direction (approx)

◄ 701132
▼ 701130

west ham united

Boleyn Ground, Green Street, Upton Park, London, E13 9AZ

website: **WWW.WHUFC.COM**
e:mail: **CUSTOMERSERVICES@WESTHAMUNITED.CO.UK**
tel no: **020 8548 2748**
colours: **CLARET AND BLUE SHIRTS, WHITE SHORTS**
nickname: **THE HAMMERS**
season 2010/11: **PREMIER LEAGUE**

Last Season: **17th** (p**38**; w**8**; d**11**; l**19**; gf**47**; ga**66**)

A difficult season for the Hammers saw Gianfranco Zola's team struggle throughout the campaign. Owned by Icelandic interests, the club's financial position was by no means secure as the fall-out – non-volcanic but equally toxic – from the collapse of the Icelandic banking system impacted early in the season. During the course of the season the club was sold to David Gold and David Sullivan, who had earlier sold Birmingham City to a Hong Kong businessman, and the new owners gave off contradictory signals in terms of their support to the manager. On the field, the club struggled and was perhaps fortunate that neither Hull City nor Burnley were able to string enough results together to threaten that one or other would survive at the Hammers' expense. A run of six straight defeats during February and March sent the club spiralling towards the drop zone and brought more serious questioning about Zola's future. However, the home victories over Sunderland and Wigan meant that, barring a mathematical disaster, the Hammers were safe once again in the Premier League. For the new season, however, the club could well again face a struggle to retain its Premier League status unless the squad is strengthened. With the season over, Zola was unceremoniously dismissed as manager; new boss Avram Grant will undoubtedly need to look to strengthen the squad significantly during the close season if the Hammers are not, once again, going to face a battle to avoid the drop.

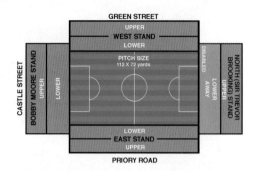

Advance Tickets Tel No: 0871 222 2700
Fax: 020 8548 2758
Training Ground: Chadwell Heath, Saville Road, Romford RM6 6DT
Brief History: Founded 1895 as Thames Ironworks, changed name to West Ham United in 1900. Former Grounds: Hermit Road, Browning Road, The Memorial Ground, moved to Boleyn Ground in 1904. Record attendance 42,322

(Total) Current Capacity: 35,303 (all seated)
Visiting Supporters' Allocation: 3,600 maximum in North (Sir Trevor Brooking) Stand
Nearest Railway Station: Barking BR, Upton Park (tube)
Parking (Car): Street parking
Parking (Coach/Bus): As directed by Police
Police Force and Tel No: Metropolitan (0300 123 1212)
Disabled Visitors' Facilities:
Wheelchairs: West Lower, Bobby Moore and Centenary Stands
Blind: Commentaries available

Anticipated Development(s): The club was taken over by former Birmingham City owners David Sullivan and David Gold in the autumn of 2009. Amongst ideas that the new owners have floated is the possibility of relocating to the Olympic Stadium being constructed for use in 2012. However, there are a number of hurdles that would need to be met before such a relocation could take place. These include the £100 million cost and the desire of the Olympic Park Legacy Co to see the ground retain an athletics track.

E Entrance(s) for visiting
supporters

1 A124 Barking Road
2 Green Street
3 North (Sir Trevor Brooking)
Stand (away)
4 Upton Park Tube Station
(¼ mile)
5 Barking station (1 mile)
6 Bobby Moore Stand
7 East Stand
8 West Stand

↑ *North direction (approx)*

◀ 701322
▼ 701332

wigan athletic

DW Stadium, Robin Park Complex, Newtown, Wigan, Lancashire, WN5 0UZ

website: **WWW.WIGANLATICS.CO.UK**
e:mail: **S.HAYTON@WIGANATHLETIC.COM**
tel no: **01942 774000**
colours: **WHITE AND BLUE SHIRTS, BLUE SHORTS**
nickname: **THE LATICS**
season 2010/11: **PREMIER LEAGUE**

Last Season: **16th** (p**38**; w**9**; d**9**; l**20**; gf**37**; ga**79**)

Under new manager Roberto Martinez, Wigan, a team now reasonably well established at Premier League level, struggled to make much of an impact in the 2009/10 season and, although never actually drawn into the relegation places, poor League form meant that fans were always conscious of the relegation zone beckoning. Fortunately, however, Portsmouth, Hull and Burnley were much poorer and so Wigan can again look forward to the Premier League in 2010/11. Away from the battle for League survival, the team's poor form was also carried through into the cup competitions, being defeated 4-1 by Blackpool at Bloomfield Road in the 2nd round of the Carling Cup and 2-0 at home by high-spending Notts County in the FA Cup 4th round replay following a 2-2 draw at the County Ground. For 2010/11, with the club again likely to lose influential players during the close season, much will depend on the quality of the players that Martinez is able to bring in. Realistically, two of the teams being promoted from the Championship – Newcastle and West Brom – look well capable of surviving in the Premier League; that means that two of the existing mid- to low-table teams could well be under threat and Wigan could well be one of those two.

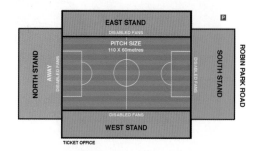

Advance Tickets Tel No: 0871 663 3552
Fax: 01942 770477
Training Ground: Christopher Park, Wigan Lower Road, Standish Lower Ground, Wigan WN6 8LB
Brief History: Founded 1932. Springfield Park used by former Wigan Borough (Football League 1921-1931) but unrelated to current club. Elected to Football League in 1978 (the last club to be elected rather than promoted). Moved to DW (JJB) Stadium for start of 1999/2000 season. Record attendance at Springfield Park 27,500; at JJB Stadium 25,133
(Total) Current Capacity: 25,138 (all seated)
Visiting Supporters' Allocation: 5,400 (maximum) in North Stand (all-seated)
Nearest Railway Stations: Wigan Wallgate/Wigan North Western (both about 1.5 miles away)
Parking (Car): 2,500 spaces at the ground
Parking (Coach/Bus): As directed
Other Clubs Sharing Ground: Wigan Warriors RLFC
Police Force and Tel No: Greater Manchester (0161 872 5050)
Disabled Visitors' Facilities:
Wheelchairs: 100 spaces
Blind: Commentaries available

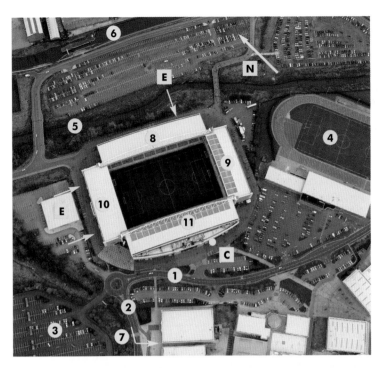

C Club Offices
E Entrance(s) for visiting
supporters

1 Loire Drive
2 Anjoy Boulevard
3 Car Parks
4 Robin Park Arena
5 River Douglas
6 Leeds-Liverpool Canal
7 To A577/A49 and Wigan
town centre plus Wigan
(Wallgate) and Wigan
(North Western) station
8 East Stand
9 South Stand
10 North Stand
11 West Stand

↑ North direction (approx)

◄ 701090
▼ 701097

wolverhampton wanderers

Molineux Ground, Waterloo Road, Wolverhampton, WV1 4QR

website: **WWW.WOLVES.CO.UK**
e:mail: **INFO@WOLVES.CO.UK**
tel no: **0871 222 2220**
colours: **GOLD SHIRTS, BLACK SHORTS**
nickname: **WOLVES**
season 2010/11: **PREMIER LEAGUE**

Last Season: **15th** (p**38**; w**9**; d**11**; l**18**; gf**32**; ga**56**)

Promoted at the end of the 2008/09 season, Mick McCarthy's Wolves were always going to be one of the pre-season favourites to make an immediate return to the Championship in the same way that they succumbed following their last campaign in the Premier League. This season, however, the team was made of sterner stuff, although the manager was to face some criticism when sending out a supposedly weaker team in those matches he felt that Wolves were unlikely to gain anything, in favour of ensuring that his key players were fit for those matches where he believed that the team might be capable of securing a decent result. It was a tactic that paid off for the most part in that the team performed sufficiently well against many of the teams that Wolves needed to defeat or draw against to gain the minimum points required for survival. Away from the League, the policy didn't always work as a 3-1 defeat in the FA Cup 4th round replay against Crystal Palace, then struggling against Administration, indicated. However, if League survival was the aim then the team achieved it; the trick will be to repeat the success in 2010/11 and, like Wigan, it's hard to escape the conclusion that Wolves could well face an uphill struggle to avoid the drop come May 2011.

Advance Tickets Tel No: 0871 222 1877
Fax: 01902 687006
Training Ground: The Sir Jack Hayward Training Ground, Douglas Turner Way, Wolverhampton WV3 9BF
Brief History: Founded 1877 as St. Lukes, combined with Goldthorn Hill to become Wolverhampton Wanderers in 1884. Former Grounds: Old Windmill Field, John Harper's Field and Dudley Road, moved to Molineux in 1889. Founder-members Football League (1888).
Record attendance 61,315
(Total) Current Capacity: 28,525 (all seated)
Visiting Supporters' Allocation: 3,200 in lower tier of Steve Bull Stand
Nearest Railway Station: Wolverhampton
Parking (Car): West Park and adjacent North Bank
Parking (Coach/Bus): As directed by Police
Police Force and Tel No: West Midlands (0345 113 5000)
Disabled Visitors' Facilities:
Wheelchairs: 104 places on two sides
Blind: Commentary (by prior arrangement)
Anticipated Developments: The club announced in late May 2010 a £40 million scheme for the expansion of Molineux, taking the ground's capacity up to 50,000. The first phase of the work, scheduled over a three-year period, is planned to encompass the demolition of the Stan Cullis and Steve Bull stands and their replacement with new two-tier structures. The next phase will be the addition of a second tier to the Jack Harris Stand. The final phase will involve the Billy Wright Stand although there is no time-frame for this as yet. During work, the ground's capacity will be significantly reduced and revised ticketing arrangements will be announced in early 2011.

C Club Offices
S Club Shop
E Entrance(s) for visiting supporters
R Refreshment bars for visiting supporters
T Toilets for visiting supporters

1 Stan Cullis Stand
2 Steve Bull Stand
3 Billy Wright Stand
4 Ring Road – St. Peters
5 Waterloo Road
6 A449 Stafford Street
7 Wolverhampton station (½ mile)
8 Jack Harris Stand
9 Molineux Street
10 Molineux Way

↑ *North direction (approx)*

◄ 703104
▼ 703109

wycombe wanderers

Adams Park, Hillbottom Road, Sands, High Wycombe, Bucks HP12 4HJ

website: **WWW.WYCOMBEWANDERERS.CO.UK**
e:mail: **WWFC@WWFC.COM**
tel no: **01494 472 100**
colours: **SKY BLUE WITH NAVY BLUE QUARTERED SHIRTS, BLUE SHORTS**
nickname: **THE CHAIRBOYS**
season 2010/11: **LEAGUE TWO**

Last season: **22nd** (relegated) (p**46**; w**10**; d**15**; l**21**; gf**56**; ga**76**)

Having guided Wycombe to promotion, Peter Taylor was to become one of the first managerial casualties in League One when he departed from the club in early October following a 1-0 home defeat against Leyton Orient that left the team deep in the drop zone. The club moved quickly to appoint Gary Waddock from Aldershot to the position of manager. However, the team continued to struggle and remained in the battle to avoid the drop right until the end of the season. A late run of form – with three wins and a draw during April – suggested an unlikely escape but the reality was that the team was never good enough to survive and relegation was confirmed following the penultimate match of the campaign – a 2-0 defeat away at Leyton Orient. Thus Wycombe face the new season back in League Two. Potentially, the club ought to be one of those vying for the Play-Offs at least but a top-half position is perhaps the best that can be hoped for.

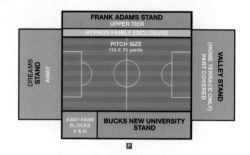

Advance Tickets Tel No: 01494 441118
Fax: 01494 527633
Training Ground: Marlow Road, Marlow, SL7 3DQ
Brief History: Founded 1884. Former Grounds: The Rye, Spring Meadows, Loakes Park, moved to Adams Park 1990. Promoted to Football League 1993. Record attendance 15,678 (Loakes Park); 10,000 (Adams Park)
(Total) Current Capacity: 10,000; (8,250 seated)
Visiting Supporters' Allocation: c2,000 in the Dreams (ex-Roger Vere) Stand
Nearest Railway Station: High Wycombe (2½ miles)
Parking (Car): At Ground and Street parking
Parking (Coach/Bus): At Ground
Other Clubs Sharing Ground: London Wasps RUFC
Police Force and Tel No: Thames Valley (0845 850 5050)
Disabled Visitors' Facilities:
Wheelchairs: Special shelter – Main Stand, Hillbottom Road end
Blind: Commentary available
Anticipated Development(s): The club's owner, Steve Hayes, who also controls London Wasps RUFC, is looking to develop a joint venture with the local council with a view to seeing a new 20,000 capacity ground in the town. If all goes according to plan, the new ground would be available by the start of thee 2014/15 season.

C Club Offices
S Club Shop
E Entrance(s) for visiting
   supporters

1 Car Park
2 Hillbottom Road
   (Industrial Estate)
3 M40 Junction 4
   (approx 2 miles)
4 Wycombe Town Centre
   (approx 2½ miles)
5 Woodlands (Frank Adams)
   Stand
6 Dreams Stand (away)
7 Valley Stand
8 Bucks New University Stand

↑ North direction (approx)

◄ 701154
▼ 701160

yeovil town

Huish Park, Lufton Way, Yeovil, Somerset, BA22 8YF

website: **WWW.YTFC.NET**
e:mail: **JCOTTON@YTFC.NET**
tel no: **01935 423662**
colours: **GREEN AND WHITE SHIRTS, WHITE SHORTS**
nickname: **THE GLOVERS**
season 2010/11: **LEAGUE ONE**

Last season: **15th** (p**46**; w**13**; d**14**; l**19**; gf**55**; ga**59**)

In Terry Skiverton's first full season as player-manager of the Glovers, Yeovil Town had a poor start to the season, winning only two of the club's first 12 League matches and being beaten 4-0 at home by Norwich City in the first round of the Carling Cup. Thereafter the club's form was patchy, but a sufficiently good run of results to lift the club up the table never materialised nor was the club ever seriously threatened with relegation, maintaining a reasonable gap between it and the drop zone for the bulk of the campaign. Relatively poor League form was, however, carried into the first round of the FA Cup where the team lost 1-0 away at non-League Oxford United. For the new season, it's likely that the Glovers will again be one of those mid-table teams that drift up and down the table but are unlikely to threaten the top spots nor, unless form deteriorates markedly, to face a battle to avoid the drop.

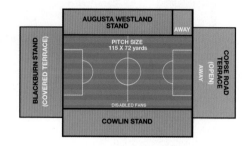

Advance Tickets Tel No: 01935 423662
Fax: 01935 847886/01935 473956
Training Ground: Adjacent to main ground
Brief History: Founded as Yeovil Casuals in 1895 and merged with Petters United in 1920. Moved to old ground (Huish) in 1920 and relocated to Huish Park in 1990. Founder members of Alliance Premier League in 1979 but relegated in 1985. Returned to Premier League in 1988 but again relegated in 1996. Promoted to the now retitled Conference in 1997 and promoted to the Nationwide League in 2003. Record Attendance: (at Huish) 16,318 (at Huish Park) 9,527
(Total) Current Capacity: 9,665; (5,212 seated)
Visiting Supporters' Allocation: 1,750 on Copse Road Terrace (open) plus limited seats in the Main (Cowlin) Stand.
Nearest Railway Station: Yeovil Junction or Yeovil Pen Mill
Parking (Car): Car park near to stadium for 800 cars
Parking (Coach/Bus): As directed
Police Force and Tel No: Avon & Somerset (0845 456 7000)
Disabled Visitors' Facilities:
Wheelchairs: Up to 20 dedicated located in the Bartlett Stand
Blind: No special facility

1 Western Avenue
2 Copse Road
3 Lufton Way
4 To town centre (one mile)
  and stations (two to four
  miles)
5 Augusta Westland Stand
6 Main (Cowlin) Stand
7 Blackburn Stand
8 Copse Road Terrace (away)
9 Memorial Road

↑ *North direction (approx)*

◂ 702784
▾ 702790

millennium stadium

Millennium Stadium, Westgate Street, Cardiff, CF10 1NS

website: **WWW.MILLENNIUMSTADIUM.COM**
e:mail: **INFO@CARDIFF-STADIUM.CO.UK**
tel no: **0870 0138600**
Fax: **029 2082 2474**
Stadium Tours: **029 208 22228**

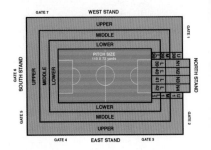

Brief History: The stadium, built upon the site of the much-loved and historic Cardiff Arms Park, was opened in 2000 and cost in excess of £100 million. As the national stadium for Wales, the ground will be primarily used in sporting terms by Rugby Union, but was used by the FA to host major fixtures (such as FA Cup and Carling Cup finals) until 2007 when the new Wembley was completed.

(Total) Current Capacity: 72,500 (all seated)

Nearest Railway Station: Cardiff Central

Parking (Car): Street parking only.

Parking (Coach/Bus): As directed by the police

Police Force and Tel No: South Wales (01656 655555)

Disabled Visitors' Facilities:

Wheelchairs: c250 designated seats. The whole stadium has been designed for ease of disabled access with lifts, etc.

Blind: Commentary available.

Anticipated Development(s): None planned